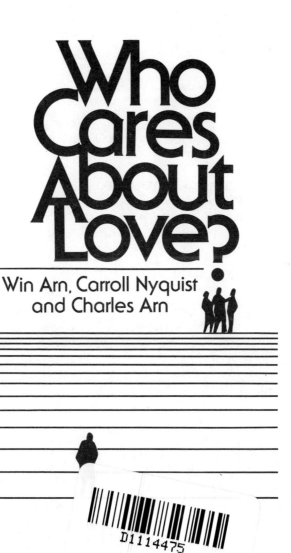

Who Cares About Love?

Win Arn, Carroll Nyquist and Charles Arn

How to bring together the
Great Commission and the Great Commandment

A stimulating and enjoyable 13-week study, entitled *Growing in Love*, is available to teach laypersons the steps of intentionally loving others. Based on the principles from this book, the course includes video, as well as complete leader's notes and participant materials. For more information contact:

Church Growth, Inc.
1921 South Myrtle Ave.
Monrovia, California 91016
1-800-423-4844

© 1986 Church Growth Press

Second printing	1987
Third printing	1988
Fourth printing	1988
Fifth printing	1990
Sixth printing	1992

Library of Congress Catalog Card No. 81-69771
ISBN 0-932208-08X

Printed in U.S.A.

Contents

Introduction

You need love. I need love. Your parents need love. Your children need love. Your friends need love. Your enemies need love. Your neighbors need love. Your employer needs love. Your employees need love. Everyone needs love. We all need love . . . and we all need to give love!

But today, there is a veritable famine that has left our world starving for love.

Whose heart has not gone out to victims of a severe drought or food shortage somewhere in the world? Mothers holding limp bodies of starving children. Bloated stomachs. Flies crawling around eyes and mouths. One must look hard just to see signs of life. Not pretty pictures, are they?

But, there's a famine much closer to home . . . a famine that destroys the inner nature of people. While people's physical bodies deteriorate and die from lack of food, people's souls deteriorate when deprived of the food vital to every human being—love.

We are in the midst of a love famine . . . that is creating starving, malnourished people right next door.

• One of every four Americans suffer from "painful loneliness."[1]

• The average marital "life expectancy" is just over 7 years, the same length of time Americans keep their automobiles.

• 50% of the children in two-parent families will see their parents divorced by the time they are 16 years old.

• 80% of the one and a half million legal abortions in the United States are obtained by unmarried women.[2]

These statistics, while grim in themselves, do not reveal the heartbreak, the tears, the hurt, the pain. Statistics don't reveal the self-doubt and rejection. Statistics don't reveal the broken lives and casualties. They don't portray the heart-wrenching pain that accompanies the love famine.

Can this love famine be checked . . . and reversed? Can individuals and churches—learn to love; and to share that love with others? The answer, we believe, is a resounding "YES!" Indeed, there are individuals, and families, and churches that *are* learning to love . . . and they are dynamically affecting the people and communities around them. The love famine, for those fortunate few, is as far away as a dark night's bad dream in the bright sunshine of the morning.

Learn to love . . . ?

Are not Christians—and churches—the bastions of love today in a troubled and loveless world? Surely, if any person—or any institution—should know and practice love, it is the Christian—and the church—whose Master taught that "God is love," and commanded "love one another."

Yet, Christians also suffer from the love famine. Divorce among Christian couples is rapidly accelerating. Christian parents see their children run away, just as do other parents. Churches split in dissension and bickering caused by an inability to love. Studies show that more people leave their churches today for lack of love than any other reason.[3]

WHO CARES ABOUT LOVE? is a book with two parts and two purposes. The first is focused on the individual Christian and church member who is called by Christ to love. It is intended to give practical insights and help for individuals to learn more about love . . . and in the process, discover how to share God's love with those around them.

The second part and purpose of WHO CARES ABOUT LOVE? is focused on the local church, which is also called by Christ to love. The second portion of this book is intended to give practical insights and help for churches to learn about love . . . and in the process, discover how to share God's love with those around them.

Who cares about love? Do today's Christians? Do today's churches? Do you?

To answer these questions, and learn more about how love is expressed and experienced in the Christian world today, we conducted a unique research study . . .

THE STUDY

The "Love/Care Quotient" (LCQ) is a measurement of love in action. Scripture tells us that "love must not be a matter of words or talk, it must be genuine and show itself in action."[4] As church growth researchers, we were interested in the relationship between a church's ability to love and its ability to reach new people and grow.

Seventeen questions were formulated and sent to churches of a variety of denominations, sizes, geographical locations, and membership growth patterns. The instructions to participating churches were to duplicate the survey, have members complete them, compile the results, and return them to us. A total of 168 churches responded from 39 denominations. The total survey represents the responses of 8658 persons.

These responses to the LCQ survey provide revealing insights into the "state of love" among Christians and American churches today. Do you know, for example, which denomination tends to have the most "loving" people—Baptist, Lutheran, or Presbyterian? In which size church do members feel most loved—small, medium, or large? Do members find more love in church committee meetings, Sunday morning Bible classes, or in small home groups? Is it harder for men or women in church to say, "I love you"?

The results of this research study, along with accompanying insights, are found throughout these chapters. You will see the special note: ■ **SURVEY RESULTS** throughout the book where an extended discussion on parts of this study is presented.

OUR ASSUMPTIONS ABOUT LOVE . . .

This book is more than just a report on a research study, it is a challenge to individual church members—and entire congregations—to intentionalize love as the central ingredient to a more meaningful and productive life. It is also a handbook on love; for within these pages you will discover practical and helpful insights, applications, and affirmations to help you and your entire church learn to love more fully. We believe that if these concepts are studied and applied, you will grow significantly in your ability to express love . . . to your family . . . to your friends . . . to your neighbors . . . to fellow members . . . to church visitors and newcomers . . . to your community . . . and your world.

To love, and to be loved . . . that is the challenge! Some people and some churches learn the secrets of love and live truly satisfying and fulfilling lives. Some search for and occasionally find love. Some live and die without ever experiencing the true meaning of love.

Within the pages of this book are assumptions we have made about love. Do you agree with them?

1. Love is the key to a fulfilled life.

It's easy to skip over this statement as simplistic, possibly trite, perhaps true only in a theoretical sense. But read it again. "Love is the key to a fulfilled life." Do you believe that? When all else fails, when other seemingly important things are gone . . . what remains and what ultimately affects lives . . . is love. Could anything, then, be more important than learning to love? We think not. Bless others and you are blessed. Give love and it is given back to you many times over. Love—receiving it, and giving it—is the secret to unlocking and experiencing life at its very fullest.

2. Love can be learned.

Behind this assumption is our conviction that both individuals and churches can increase their ability to love. The Apostle Paul assumed love could be learned when he encouraged the Thessalonians to " . . . make your love increase and overflow, for each other and for everyone else . . . "[5] An individual's and a church's love-ability can be improved . . . and should be! At the same time, we recognize that doing so is not easy. In fact, learning to love can be one of the greatest and most difficult challenges of your life. But with the greatest challenges come the greatest rewards.

3. Christ wants us to love.

Jesus instructed his followers again and again . . . "Love one another,"[6] "Love your neighbor as yourself,"[7] "Love your enemies,"[8] "Greater love has no one than one lay down his life for his friends,"[9] "My command is this: love each other as I have loved you . . . you are my friends if you do what I command . . . this is my command: love each other."[10] Later Christ said that all the law and the prophets can be put simply into two commandments; first, to love God with all your heart; and second, to love your neighbor as yourself.[11] Of all the commands in the Bible, "to love" is given the most often. There was *nothing* more important to Christ than for His followers to love.

4. The source of love is God.

"God is love"[12] . . . and as people are directly in touch with the Author and Creator of love, they are enabled . . . empowered . . . to be more effective in loving. This link with the Source becomes the extra "plus" for practicing the power of love. Individuals who have a relationship with their Creator have an inexhaustible source of love. Love is a fruit of the spirit which comes from the very essence of our creator " . . . because God has given us the Holy Spirit to fill our hearts with love."[13]

WHO IS "CHUCK BRADLEY"?

You may have already met Chuck Bradley through one of many films.[14] Perhaps you are familiar with this lovable layperson through the popular book *THE MASTER'S PLAN FOR MAKING DISCIPLES.*[15] You may have studied the video instruction tape in THE MASTER'S PLAN Church Action Kit.[16] Chuck is also featured in the popular film series entitled WHO CARES ABOUT LOVE? which follows the storyline of this book.[17] If you have previously met Chuck, you will enjoy this next saga, based on a true story about love.

If Chuck is a stranger to you, we believe you will come to like him. He's a nice sort of guy. He may not be the one in his church with the greatest spiritual depth. Chuck is not a master teacher or charismatic leader. But he is a lot like most of us. He tries to be honest with himself and others. He wants to learn to grow in his Christian life.

Why is Chuck Bradley in this book?

Because we believe, in many ways, Chuck typifies all of us. He helps us to see ourselves . . . our struggles . . . our failures . . . our victories. With Chuck, we're not as alone. With his help, we can learn about love without bumping our heads.

Chuck also helps us to laugh at ourselves. He helps us see the brighter side of love . . . and life. He helps us in our understandings about love. We can struggle with Chuck . . . and together with him, learn about love.

"If I Only Lived Closer to the Famine . . . "

Chuck Bradley had not intended to watch the entire television program. But the images had been so compelling

and powerful that he had been unable to turn the set off. It was a documentary on famine in a third world country, complete with gripping images of starving people, many only hours away from death.

When the appeal for financial assistance was given, Chuck carefully copied down the phone number. He intended to respond with a contribution, because he felt that such a desperate need deserved all the help people who believed in Jesus Christ could give.

At the end of the program, Chuck turned off the TV and went outside. It would be some time before he could forget those images of human suffering. "If I only lived closer to the famine," Chuck said to himself, "I'm sure I would do more than just mail in a check."

Outside the sky was blue. The air . . . fresh and clean. Birds sang contentedly. Down the street Chuck heard the voices of happy children. What a contrast from those parts of the world where children never live to play.

This peaceful atmosphere was rudely broken with the intrusive sound of a loud, noisy motorcycle driven by a well-muscled young man in a black leather jacket. The rider and his machine pulled into the driveway next door to Chuck's house. After turning off the ignition, Chuck's new neighbor looked over in his direction.

But Chuck gave no response. He didn't care for motorcycles . . . or motorcycle people. They definitely were not his type. And Chuck didn't generally bother to initiate relationships among people with whom he had nothing in common.

What Chuck did not realize was that this neighbor, living right next door, had a need every bit as real, and as devastating, as the starving and malnourished children he had just seen on television. His neighbor, Ken Martin, needed love. Indeed . . . he was starving for love!

YOU CAN BE GOD'S "LOVE OASIS"

In the midst of this love-famine is a great untapped reservoir of love—the church. Hidden deep in the souls of most Christians and churches is the answer to the love famine. Yet, in many churches, this love potential goes untapped . . . buried somewhere beneath the business, the bureaucracy, the by-laws, and the bulletins of the modern congregation. WHO CARES ABOUT LOVE? was written to begin removing this outer crust of diversionary "busy-ness" that can easily inhibit love. It was written to help release the love in your life, and your church's life, to a famished world.

Can the followers of Jesus Christ become an oasis of living water—a bubbling spring of life flowing into a love-starved community that needs to taste the fresh, cool measure of God's love?

Is the love we sing of in our hymns and speak of in our sermons only a mirage that vanishes when the thirsty come to drink? Or, is it a tangible love that grows purer, richer, and deeper, the more we drink from its Source?

What about you and me? Do we model the kind of love, for our thirsty and starving neighbors, that reflects God's love?

You can be God's love oasis in the midst of this love famine! Get involved. Learn the principles of love. Then begin to apply them right where you are—in your family, on your job, in your church, at your club, with your neighbors. When you do, you will find that a joy comes with it of miraculous dimensions . . . for others and for yourself. You will see changes in the people around you, as well as changes in yourself. Your relationships with family members, work associates, church members and visitors, friends, and neighbors will blossom and grow . . . because you have become God's instrument—his oasis of love—for them.

Let's begin the adventure!

Footnotes

1. Fred Smith, CHRISTIANITY TODAY "The Gift of Greeting" Dec. 13, 1985, Vol. 29, No. 18, p. 70.
2. Statistical references from: "The Changing American Family" by Arland Thornton, *Population Bulletin* Vol. 38, No. 4.
3. Warren J. Hartman, *A Study of the Church School in the United Methodist Church* (Nashville: Board of Education, 1972), p. 54.
4. I Jn. 3:18 (New English)
5. I Thessalonians 3:12
6. John 13:35
7. Matthew 19:19
8. Matthew 5:44
9. John 15:13
10. John 15:12,14,17
11. Matthew 22:37-39, Mark 12:30-31
12. I John 4:8,16
13. Romans 5:5 (Living Bible)
14. These films, featuring "Chuck Bradley," were produced by Dr. Win Arn and written/directed by Mr. Carroll Nyquist. A complete catalog of these and other excellent films/videos is available from Church Growth, 1921 S. Myrtle Ave., Monrovia, CA 91016.
15. Win Arn and Charles Arn. *The Master's Plan for Making Disciples* (Pasadena: Church Growth Press, 1982). This book is available from Church Growth in Pasadena, CA. See footnote 14.
16. *THE MASTER'S PLAN* Church Action Kit is one of the finest evangelism training resources available for laypersons. Descriptive information is available from Church Growth, Monrovia, CA
17. The film series WHO CARES ABOUT LOVE? is available from Church Growth, or most religious film libraries.

CHAPTER ONE

Learning to Love

"It is possible that a man can be so changed by love as hardly to be recognized as the same person." Terence

Is it possible for us to love more fully?

. . . to love others as we, ourselves, would like to be loved?

To love the way Christ showed us to love?

Is it possible for our churches to love more fully?

To *really practice* Christ-like love? . . . to "love one another"? . . . to "love our neighbors"?

Many persons today feel inadequately prepared to express or share love. The reasons are varied. Some are handicapped because they grew up in homes where love was seldom shown. Others are currently living in partial or splintered families where love seems to have already failed. Some have been hardened by past rejections, and their ability to love has become seriously impaired. Whatever the reasons, most of us find it difficult to express love.

An experiment was recently conducted in which individuals were given the assignment of approaching persons whom they loved, and verbally expressing that love to them. Almost all participants reported they felt tongue-tied . . . ill-at-ease . . . awkward . . . embarrassed. Some could not even complete the assignment.[1] In discussing their experiences after the assignment, participants agreed that "it was strange, indeed, that so many found it threatening to communicate love!" The researcher went on to observe that, "it then became obvious why we hear the voice of love so seldom, and when it is heard it is spoken so softly, so shyly. This is true even though we have learned that unexpressed love is the greatest cause of our sorrow and regrets."[2]

While the love famine ravages the secular world, it leaves its mark on churches, as well. Today people are *leaving* their churches for lack of love . . .

A wide-ranging study[3] interviewed members who had recently dropped out of their church, and found that the majority of persons said that they left their church because they did not feel needed, wanted, or loved. People need to be loved, even in the church . . . *especially* in the church.

■ SURVEY RESULTS

A question on the Love/Caring Quotient (LCQ) Survey focused on love experienced by Christians today—where do they find it? At home, at church, at school, work, in social activities?

Question: "On a scale of 1-10, how 'loved' do you feel by the following persons: spouse, parents, other family, pastor, other church members, close friends, neighbors, school/work associates?" See the results on page 17.

Interesting insights can be found here. As would be expected, people feel most loved by "spouse" and "parents." If, and when, people experience love, it is most often found in the family. Yet, if little or no love is experienced from a spouse or parents, there seems to be no place—including the church—where a comparable kind of love

How Loved we Feel

ON A SCALE OF
1-10 HOW LOVED
DO YOU FEEL BY
THE FOLLOWING
PERSONS?

5.2	Neighbors
5.6	School work Associates
6.6	Church Members
7.6	Pastor — Close Friends
8.3	Family
8.7	Parents
9.0	Spouse

can be found. Notice that most people rated the love they received from church members a rather week 6.6 (on a scale of 1-10), only one point better than from casual associates and neighbors.

If it is true that love expressed among members toward each other is relatively low, how much love do you suppose non-members experience from people in the church? And what about the love experienced by church visitors? The fact is, most churches are not seen by outsiders as a place to find genuine love and caring. According to our LCQ Survey (the first systematic study of love in the local church), most church members are little more than acquaintances to each other. And visitors experience significantly less love than even members. The community generally goes unloved.

In Christian theory, we are to love one another; in actual practice, this commandment of Christ seems to receive a low priority. We need to learn how to love, or how to love again.

Is it possible to change . . . to grow . . . to learn to love? Absolutely! It begins as we take an honest look at our past, our present, and our future . . .

A STORY ABOUT LOVE—FOR ALL SEASONS

There is a wonderful story by Charles Dickens, told and retold at the Christmas season, which tells of the transformation of Ebenezer Scrooge from a cold and self-centered tightwad to a generous, loving man.

It is Christmas eve. We meet Ebenezer Scrooge—as unloving a man as ever one could be. Nothing moves him to care. Nothing moves him to joy. Nothing seems to move him at all, except his money. Ebenezer Scrooge has forgotten how to love.

The story begins early in the evening as Scrooge is visited by the ghost of his former business partner, Jacob Marley. The ghost has come to tell Scrooge there is more to life than his money and his business . . . and there is still time to change. But Scrooge ignores his old partner's words of experience with a "Bah . . . humbug!" and goes off to bed.

Three other ghosts visit Ebenezer on that Christmas eve . . . the ghost of the past, the present, and the future. Each one brings a powerful message of love.

The ghost of "Christmas past" takes Ebenezer back to an earlier time in his life when he had, indeed, known the joy of love. His family had been poor, and Ebenezer had few of the clothes or toys that other children owned. But he remembered one Christmas when his mother had given up many of her own needs to buy little Ebenezer the bicycle he had dreamed about. His mother's love left an indelible impression on Ebenezer. But that was a long time ago, and the flicker of love seems to have been snuffed out over the years.

The ghost of "Christmas past" then takes Ebenezer to a time when he had once loved a beautiful girl. They were engaged to be married, but Ebenezer's priorities had begun to change. When his mother died, he had determined never to be as poor as his family had been. And when forced to choose between the pursuit of money and a caring relationship with the young girl, Ebenezer had turned away from love.

The second visit Scrooge receives this evening is from the ghost of "Christmas present," who shows Ebenezer two models of real love. Their first visit is to the home of his nephew, Fred. Earlier that day his nephew had invited Uncle Ebenezer to a Christmas party, but Scrooge had wanted no part of it. Now as an unseen observer, Scrooge hears words of spite from others at the party about him and his loveless attitude. But Fred refuses to let his friends speak disdainfully of his uncle. There is love in the young man's heart, even for the unlovely Ebenezer Scrooge.

Next, the ghost takes Scrooge to the home of his employee, Bob Cratchit, and his wife and four children, including the crippled Tiny Tim. The family is excitedly preparing their meager Christmas dinner and anticipating the few homemade presents under their small tree. What Scrooge sees in the Cratchit family is something he has not experienced since he was a young boy—love. The family loves each other and cares for each other. Bob Cratchit is a model of love and caring even for his gruff and stingy employer, though his wife and children speak unkindly of "that tightwad Scrooge." The father sees the best in Scrooge, while the readers of Dickens' story know there is precious little in the old man to love. But in the spirit of love, Bob Cratchit leads his family in a prayer: "God bless us every one; yes, even Mr. Scrooge."

Ebenezer's discovery about love is not yet over. A third ghost visits his bedside that evening, the ghost of "Christmas future." Ebenezer is taken on a journey into the probable future, again to the home of Bob Cratchit. On this visit, however, he finds an empty chair at the table and a small cane hanging unused on the wall. The family was unable to pay for the operation the young boy needed, and Tiny Tim had died.

The next stop on Scrooge's journey into the future is to the cemetery and the grave of young Tiny Tim. Ebenezer is learning that life is very short, and the seemingly important things of today are of little consequence when one faces death. The ghost then takes Scrooge to another part of the cemetery where he brushes away the snow and sees a tombstone marked: "Ebenezer Scrooge." "Spirit!" the old man cries out. "Is this the way it will be, or only the way it might be?"

But as we all remember, the story has a happy ending. Ebenezer Scrooge wakes the next morning to discover that it is Christmas day! He begins the exhilarating process, which we know will last the rest of his life, of setting right his years of love lost. It's a joyful time for everyone . . . for the Cratchit family and Tiny Tim, who receive the money for the operation; for Scrooge's nephew, who finds his uncle a new person who loves and gives; for the reader, who vicariously shares the joy of a changed life; and for Ebenezer Scrooge, who discovers love and the joy of sharing it.

What a story of learning to love!

While the setting of the story is the Christmas season, learning to love can happen at any season . . . to any person who reflects on his/her life, and like Ebenezer Scrooge, determines to change . . . to grow . . . and to learn to love.

"Do You Know Anything About the Subject?"

It was a lazy, warm summer afternoon. Chuck was dozing pleasantly in a lounge chair in his back yard. Prince, his motorcycling neighbor's large, friendly dog bounded into the yard and awakened Chuck with a bark and a friendly lick on the face.

"Hey, get out of here! Go on!"

Prince, however, did not respond to his orders and continued licking Chuck's face. Chuck rolled out of his chair and tried unsuccessfully to chase the dog away. Prince circled playfully, enjoying the game.

"Go home! Scat! Get out of here!" Chuck clapped his hands and ushered the dog to the edge of his yard.

Out of breath, Chuck returned to his lounge chair, intent on resuming his interrupted nap. Just short of his destination he felt his foot slip along the ground. Chuck looked at the bottom of his right shoe. "Yuk."

The sound of a large motorcycle prompted Chuck to look over the fence as Ken Martin rode into his driveway and dismounted. The cyclist seemed formidable in his tightly fitting black leather jacket. His dog, Prince, ran over and welcomed him.

Chuck watched as Ken, an obvious dog lover, returned the welcome.

"Chuck, what are you doing?" Diane, Chuck's wife, came up beside him, carrying a package.

"Oh, our new neighbor's dog was back."

"I thought you were going to talk to him about keeping his dog on a leash."

"Diane, it would just be a waste of time."

"How do you know?" asked Diane. "Have you ever tried to get acquainted?"

"No, I haven't."

Diane was surprised. "You mean, in the two months since he moved in, you haven't even said 'hello' to him?"

Chuck looked over at his neighbor who was enjoying a bottle of beer as he tinkered with his motorcycle. "Diane, he's just not my type." In an effort to change the subject, Chuck pointed to the opened package in Diane's hand. "What's that?"

"It looks like a video tape from church for the Love Seminar coming up."

"Good. I've been expecting that."

"You have?" asked Diane. "Chuck, does this mean you're *leading the seminar?*"

"That's right," answered Chuck. "Don't you approve?"

"Well, I was really looking forward to this seminar. I wanted to learn something about love."

"And if I'm the leader, that won't happen?"

"Well," asked Diane, "do you know anything about the subject?"

"Do I know anything about the subject?" Chuck paused for emphasis. "Diane, if there's one subject I know something about, it's love."

"Sweetheart, you do realize what kind of love we'll be talking about?"

"Of course I do. The kind of love that's in the Bible. 'God so loved the world . . .' and that sort of thing."

Diane was still unconvinced. "And you really know about that?"

"Sure. I know all the verses . . . and all the principles."

"Oh, you do, do you?" Diane's eyes twinkled as she added, "Then you know the verse that says, 'love your neighbor . . . even if he rides a motorcycle'?"

"Diane, you know there's no such verse in the Bible. And besides," Chuck gestured in Ken's direction, "I'm sure God doesn't really expect us to love everybody."

"Well, I wouldn't know," said Diane, giving Chuck a playful kiss before turning to walk away, "I'm not the seminar leader."

WHAT IS LOVE?

A Practical Working Definition

When we are commanded to "*love* one another," or to *love* our neighbors, or to *love* our enemies—what is meant by the word "love"?

The classic discussion on the characteristics of love is found in the Apostle Paul's first letter to the Corinthians. Hailed as a masterpiece on love, Chapter 13 provides beautiful insight into the practical meaning of love. It should be read in its entirety by all of us . . . and often. In this chapter we discover . . .

What love is (and does)
- is patient
- is kind
- searches for truth
- holds up under pressure
- always believes the best
- looks to the future, not the past
- is consistent

What love is not (and does not)
- is not jealous
- does not brag
- does not embarrass others
- is not arrogant
- is not selfish
- does not remember a wrong suffered
- does not anger easily

Paul concludes by saying, "Now abides faith, hope, love . . . but the greatest is love."[4]

But while Paul describes well the characteristics of love, he does not precisely define it.[5] In seeking our own definition of love, we have tried to identify the very basic nature of love found in Scripture . . . in God's love . . . as modeled by Christ, Himself:

"For God so *loved* the world that He gave His only Son . . ."[6]

"But God demonstrates his own *love* for us in this: While we were still sinners, Christ died for us."[7]

"The greatest *love* shown is when a person lays down his life for his friends."[8]

By using these and other Scriptures, we give you our definition of love which will be used throughout the remainder of this book:

"Love is intentionally doing something caring or helpful for another person, in Jesus' name, regardless of the cost or consequence to oneself."

Let's consider the key words and phrases of this definition . . .

"intentionally" Love does not happen by accident. Love happens because it is planned and premeditated. Love is determining to act in a particular way.

"doing something" Love is action. If it is not seen, or observed, or experienced on a regular basis, there is cause to doubt whether it is really love. "Let's stop just saying we love people; let us really love them and show it by our actions."[9]

"caring" This word is most often and obviously seen in parents' caring for their children. The ultimate caring for a person (defined in the dictionary as "a feeling of concern and protection"[10]) is in giving one's own life to protect the object of one's love. "We know Christ's love for us in that he gave his life. Therefore, we ought also give our lives for our brethren."[11]

"helpful" The word means "lend strength to." Where a need exists, love responds. Whereas one person is weak, two are strong.[12] Love builds up the other person. Love makes up for the person's weakness in certain areas through the strength of the other. "When you have done it for the least of these my brethren, you have done it to me."[13]

"for another person" Love is always focused on a person/s. Love does not exist in a vacuum. Self-interest is not what motivates action. The well-being and interest of the person who is loved motivates action.

"in Jesus' name" What is meant by this phrase? Christ, Himself, tells us to pray "in my name."[14] Is the phrase some magic formula to guarantee an answered prayer, or an "inside track" to God? No. "In Jesus' name" means that we are praying, or doing an act of love, in the spirit of Jesus Christ . . . with the same motivation that Christ would have done that caring act. In Jesus' name, is our motivation of the same attitude of love, risk, sacrifice, obedience, and unconditional giving that we see in Christ.

"regardless of the cost or consequence to one-self." True love puts others ahead of oneself. It does not say, "I love you if it doesn't cost anything . . . or if it's convenient . . . or if I don't hurt myself in the process." Can you imagine God putting those conditions on His love for us? "Be imitators of God, therefore, as dearly loved children and live a life of love, just as Christ loved us and gave himself up for us as a fragrant offering and sacrifice to God."[15]

"How Can You Love Someone You Don't Even Like?"

Chuck was beginning his initial preparation for leading his church's Love Seminar. He loaded a cassette into his video player, pushed the "PLAY" button, and settled back to watch.

The video came to life and the narrator began . . .

"First of all, what are the principle characteristics of love as presented in the New Testament?" The narrator paused. "First, New Testament love is more than words or promises . . . it is action. Second, love is always intentional, never accidental."

Surrounded by notepads, manuals, and workbooks, Chuck listened and took notes.

"Do you remember the story Jesus told when he was teaching about love?" the video narrator asked. "It was of the Good Samaritan and the loving acts he did for the man on the Jericho road." Chuck nodded slightly. "The Samaritan not only bandaged the man's wounds, but he took him to an inn where he could be cared for. This is a good illustration of New Testament love, which we define as, 'intentionally doing something caring or helpful for another person, in Jesus' name, regardless of the cost or consequences to oneself.' That's the way God

loves us, and He wants us to do the same for others."

Chuck pushed the video player to "PAUSE" and made some notes. As he did, his concentration was interrupted by the sound of loud rock music from next door. He walked to the kitchen window and opened it. The music was even louder. Mixed with the music were sounds of a large boisterous party. Chuck shook his head, slammed the window, and went to the phone. He was definitely irritated.

"Operator, get me the police!"

"Sweetheart, is that being a good neighbor?" Diane had come in from the next room.

"Diane, our motorcycling neighbor is having a wild party," answered Chuck. "Who knows what kind of people are there? Or, what sort of things they're doing?"

"But, Chuck," asked Diane, "is that a good Christian testimony? Calling the police?"

Chuck hung up the phone. "So, what am I supposed to do . . . turn the other cheek?"

"*I just think you should love your neighbor,*" *replied Diane.* "*Even if you don't like him.*"

At first, Chuck thought Diane's comment was ridiculous. How can you love someone you don't like? But later, Chuck discovered the verse where Jesus said, "*Love your enemies, do good to those who hate you, bless those who curse you, pray for those who treat you badly.*" And, if that wasn't plain enough, Jesus also said, "*If you love only those who love you, what credit is that to you? Even the sinners love those who love them!*"

That gave Chuck something to think about. "*When it comes to loving people,*" he wondered, "*do I only love those who love me back? And . . . can I really love my enemies?*"

Footnotes

1. Leo Buscaglia, *Loving Each Other* (Thorofare, NJ: Slack Inc., 1984), p. 54.
2. Op. cit., p. 54.
3. Warren Hartman, *Membership Trends: A Study of Growth and Decline in the United Methodist Church* (Nashville: Discipleship Resources, 1976).
4. I Corinthians 13:13
5. Gary Inrig, *Quality Friendship* (Chicago: Moody Press, 1981), p. 156.
6. I John 3:16
7. Romans 5:8
8. John 15:13
9. I John 3:18
10. The Random House Dictionary of the English Language (New York: Random House, 1968), p. 204.
11. I John 3:16
12. Ecclesiastes 4:10
13. Matthew 25:40
14. John 14:13-14
15. Ephesians 5:1-2

CHAPTER TWO

Why Love?

*"They are the true disciples of Christ,
not who know most, but who love most."*
Spanheim

Pause for a moment . . . and reflect on some of
the people who have loved you.

Was it your mother, who put her own needs aside and
thought first of your health and happiness?

Was it a friend, who today is hundreds of miles away,
but whose bond of love is still like a warm, glowing ember?

Was it a person whose caring concern and love for you
came as a total surprise in a time of need?

Was it a pastor, whose special Christ-like love extended
beyond mere professional duty?

Or, was it your spouse who, for better or for worse, was
there when you most needed support?

You were loved! You were important! You mattered to
someone. You didn't need to make false pretenses. You
didn't have to hide who you were, or how you felt. You
laughed together. You cried together. You grew in love

together. It's a joy just to remember, isn't it? To be loved is one of the most fulfilling experiences in life.

But . . . to love others is even more fulfilling and rewarding!

1. Why love? Because we are loved.

God loves you! Breathe deeply and let this truth roll around inside you. God loves you! His love for you is so great that He sent His own Son to die for you. GOD LOVES YOU!

Set in the mountains of West Virginia, a moving story illustrates the great love God has for you and me, and the sacrifice He made because of love . . . [1]

A young father, his wife, and their 4-year-old son lived in a small house on the bank of the Ohio River, a few hundred yards from a nearby railroad bridge. The father's responsibility was to see that the bridge was secure for the passenger trains which crossed four times a day. Because barges and ships frequently used the river, the railroad bridge had been built to pivot on a center mooring in the middle of the river. When not in use, the bridge was positioned up and down the river, allowing boats to pass. Fifteen minutes before each train arrived, the young man would throw the power switch which moved the bridge across the river, connecting the tracks on each bank. When the train had safely crossed, he would return the bridge back for river traffic to pass.

One summer afternoon, 15 minutes prior to the arrival of the next train, the father threw the switch and watched the bridge move slowly around, and finally stop at the river bank. But the small light next to the switch, which normally turned from red to green when the bridge was locked in place, did not appear. The red light kept flashing, and suddenly the warning bell sounded, indicating something was wrong. The man ran over to the end of the bridge. He looked down and saw a 6-inch gap where the tracks from the bridge had not aligned with the tracks on land.

In such an emergency, the man had been trained to use a special tool to insert in the locking device, and manually pull the tracks together for the train to cross. He ran to the storage box next to the tracks, removed the 4-foot steel bar, and inserted it in place. His muscles strained against the heavy bar as the tracks moved slowly toward each other and into place. The warning bell stopped as the man heard the whistle from the approaching train signalling it was entering the final curve prior to the river.

Straining to hold the steel rod in position, the father waited.

Suddenly, he looked down the tracks, and his heart jumped. Several hundred yards away, running toward him, was his 4-year-old son, arms outstretched, laughing and shouting "Daddy, Daddy."

The father leaped up to run and snatch his son from the tracks. At the same time he heard the loud warning bell begin to sound. He looked down to see the tracks had separated. The awful realization rushed over him. There was not time to reach his son and return to keep the bridge in position before the approaching train reached the river.

The father knew he must make a decision.

On board the train were people on their way to work, children playing in the aisles, women reading their newspapers, couples watching the scenery. None of them knew the young father. But if they had been looking out the window as the train came speeding onto the bridge that day, they would have seen a young man just a few inches from the train, straining to hold back a steel bar as tears were streaming down his face. None realized the gift of life they had just been given, or the sacrifice the father had made on their behalf.

Is this story not a vivid illustration of God's love for us? "For God so loved the world that He gave His only Son . . ."[2] —that we might have life.

GOD LOVES YOU!

2. Why love? Because we were created to love.

Scripture teaches that God is love.[3] The very *essence* of our Maker is love. We also learn that we are created in the image of God.[4] Thus, ingrained and implanted deep inside our very inner natures is that essence of the Creator . . . love. When we love, we activate that inner spiritual nature, and become more like our maker. We set in motion one of the megapowers in God's universe.

"Someday, after we have mastered the winds, the waves, the tides, and gravity, we will harness for God the energies of love and then for the second time in the history of the world, man will have discovered fire."[5]

In the philosopher Plato's classic story, "The Myth of the Cave," we can see a parable on the discovery of love, and the fulness to life it was meant to bring. The story tells of a group of people who had spent their entire lives chained to the inside of a cold, dark cave. Their only knowledge of life outside was from the shadows cast on the cave's wall in front of them by the people and objects outside. Then, one day a man escaped from the cave. What he saw outside amazed him. He saw color . . . shapes . . . dimension. He saw light and what caused the shadows. He saw the sky and the water. The clouds. The birds.

It was such an unbelievable new reality that he had to return and tell his friends in the cave of this new world outside. But those in the cave did not understand. Reality, for them, was seen as shadows on the wall. The idea of another world beyond their limited experience could not be real. So the man left, saddened that his friends could not understand the truth.

Some people's perceptions and experiences of love are limited to shadows in their loveless cave. But as we learn to love, we free ourselves from our chains of ignorance, and experience the completeness of a new reality which lies beyond the walls of our cave. Through loving, we become more complete and fulfilled. We experience the joy and fulness of life which God placed in life for those who are able to discover it.

3. Why love? Because others need our love.

An older woman recently confided, "I'm all alone and I don't know what to do. I don't think anyone cares about me anymore. No one asks me to go out, calls me, or writes. I've outlived all of my friends. My family is gone away. I'm afraid to be alone."[6]

This woman was simply verbalizing what everyone fears . . . not being loved.

Old or young, single or married, Christian or non-Christian . . . everyone needs love.

Research over the past ten years has conclusively shown a relationship between being loved and being healthy. One recent study found that persons who live alone, and have few or no close friends, have a mortality rate equal to regular cigarette smokers.[7] It has been discovered that people without loving support in time of sickness take longer to recover. In serious cases, those without the caring support of friends and family die more often than patients who know their lives have value to others. One research physician at Johns Hopkins calls loneliness the number one killer—"some other illness goes on the death certificate, but the prime cause was loneliness."[8]

In his best-selling book MEGATRENDS, John Naisbitt observes that we are in a new and uncertain era of human civilization, which he calls "high tech."[9] Naisbitt suggests that coping with this high tech society requires a "high touch" response: "Today, more than ever, there is an increased need to be in touch with people. We must learn to balance the material wonders of technology with the spiritual demands of our human nature."[10] As society becomes more and more depersonalized, the need of people to be with others, and to be close to others, becomes more and more important.

We all need help from others . . . it is basic to our survival. We simply can't make it on our own. The human being has the longest "dependency" period of any living organism. We begin life in need. We never completely outgrow it.

The people closest to you—your friends and family—have love needs. Some of them have special needs right now, even as you are reading this book. Their needs may be for *encouragement,* as they face new and uncertain challenges in their lives. Love gives encouragement. Perhaps their needs are for *affirmation,* as they face questions of their personal value and self-worth. Love gives affirmation. At times their needs are *material;* at other times, *emotional;* and still other occasions, *spiritual.* Your love can help meet their needs.

There is a super-natural quality in the power of love. It brings hope to the hopeless. It brings strength to the weak. It brings life to the dying. Are there not times when we all need help? Love is what friends, family, church members, visitors, work associates, neighbors need when they hurt, when they stumble and fall. Love heals, love upholds, love restores.

4. Why love? Because God wants us to love.

"Dear friends, since God so loved us, we also ought to love one another. No one has ever seen God; but if we love each other, God lives in us and his love is made complete in us."[11]

In loving, we return God's love.

The entire New Testament is a love story . . . of His love for us. "For God so loved . . . " you!

So . . . how do we respond to God's love? "The Great Commandment" tells us to love the Lord God with all our heart, mind, and soul. But how do we do that? How do we actually love God?

Do we repeat endlessly the words, "God, I love you!

God, I love you"? Do we sit in a dark room trying to stir up warm and affectionate feelings toward God? Is that what loving him really means?

Remember our definition of love? *Love is doing something caring or helpful for another person, in Jesus' name, regardless of the cost or consequence to oneself.* Love goes beyond feelings. Love is action.

Loving God means showing it, not just saying it. Loving God means loving your brother . . . loving your neighbor . . . loving fellow Christians . . . even loving your enemy. Those who say they love God but don't love their brother, according to the Bible,[12] do not really love God. That's serious business!

In the next few chapters, we will be sharing insights into working at love and making love work.

"Dear friends, since God so loved us, we also ought to love one another . . . if we love each other, God lives in us and His love is made complete in us."[13]

"What If I Get a Low Score . . . ?"

With a hot pad, Chuck gingerly removed a TV dinner from the oven and carried it into the family room. Tonight he was dining alone since Diane was away at a Women's Church retreat.

To give himself company as he ate, Chuck pushed the "PLAY" button to watch more of the Love Seminar video.

"Why is it important to love one another and to love our neighbors?" asked the video narrator. "Why did God command us to do this?

The answer is, that it's part of His plan for loving the world. God wants His disciples to serve as 'channels' through which His love can flow to others. We're to be 'delivery systems' for God's love. And, if we fail to do that, many needy people will be deprived of His love."

Chuck took a few more bites of his TV dinner.

"Also, when God's people genuinely love each other and love their neighbors, they attract men and women to Christ and His church," continued the narrator. "Is the love in your life attracting lost men and women to Jesus Christ?"

Chuck wasn't sure how to answer that question.

"Scripture says we should make love our aim. Is love your aim?"

This question made Chuck feel slightly uncomfortable.

"To help you find out how loving you are, we've prepared a personal 'Love/Caring Inventory,' which you will find in your workbook. At this time, please stop the video and answer the questions in this survey."

Chuck found the sheet and examined it. But after looking at some of the questions, he was hesitant to begin.

"What if I get a low score? How would that look for the seminar leader?" Chuck came up with a happier thought. "But maybe I'll get a good score . . . I'd certainly get good marks as a husband . . . in fact, I think Diane is pretty lucky to have me. I'm kind and considerate. I'm a good provider . . . "

His thoughts were interrupted by the front doorbell.

Ken Martin, Chuck's neighbor, was waiting as he opened the door.

"Hi, I'm Ken Martin, from next door. Do you know a doctor we could call? My wife, Chris, has these terrible stomach pains . . . and she's been throwing up a lot and . . . "

Chuck's phone rang inside.

"Excuse me, Ken, I've got to answer that. I'll be right back."

Chuck made a hasty exist, leaving Ken wondering what to do.

Inside, Chuck picked up the phone. "Hello . . . Oh, hi, Diane. How's the retreat going? . . . Some of your friends had a nice little birthday party for you this afternoon?"

Had he forgotten Diane's birthday again? Obviously!

"Oh, Happy Birthday, Sweetheart . . . No, uh, I didn't really forget your birthday . . . uh, but what I did forget

was to send your present with you. Uh, . . . that's what I
forgot. But, it'll be right here . . . uh, waiting for you,
when you get home tomorrow."

The doorbell rang again.

"Oh no! I left him standing at the door. Diane, I've got
to go . . . Who? Well, our next door neighbor. His wife is
sick and he's looking for a doctor . . . Of course, I'll try to
be a good neighbor . . . Yeah, see you tomorrow . . . I love
you, too."

Chuck hung up the phone and hurried back to the
door. But there was no one waiting. He stepped outside
and looked around, but his neighbor had gone. With a
shrug Chuck returned to the video on love.

Footnotes

1. A 12-minute color film, entitled *The Sacrifice,* has been produced
   which depicts this story. Available from Brigham Young University.
2. John 3:16
3. I John 4:8
4. Genesis 1:26
5. Pierre Teilhard De Chardin, In *Unconditional Love* by John Powell (Allen, TX:
   Argus Communications, 1978), p. 97.
6. Leo Buscaglia, *Loving One Another* (Thorofare, NJ: Slack, Inc., 1984), p. 20.
7. Sheila Sobell Maramarco. "Friendship: The Tie That Binds You in Good
   Health," in PSA Magazine, January 1983, p. 32-34.
8. Fred Smith, *Christianity Today,* "The Gift of Greeting." Vol. 29, No. 18, p. 70.
9. John Naisbitt, *Megatrends* (New York: Warner Books, 1982).
10. Op. Cit. p. 40.
11. I John 4:11-12
12. I John 4:20
13. I John 4:11-12

CHAPTER THREE

Why We Fail at Love

*"Love is the hardest lesson in Christianity;
but for that reason it should be
most our care to learn it."* William Penn

"Isn't It the Thought That Counts?"

*Late the next day, Chuck drove into his driveway and got
out of the car with a large gift-wrapped package. He
hoped Diane had not yet arrived.*

*Suddenly he heard a bark and turned around just as
his neighbor's large, friendly dog jumped up trying to
lick him on the face. In maneuvering to avoid the dog,
Chuck nearly dropped the package.*

*"Go home, Prince! If you make me break this, I'm in
big trouble."*

*The dog, barking happily, followed him to the front
door where Chuck just managed to get inside without
letting the dog in behind. Chuck leaned against the door
and paused to catch his breath.*

*"Hi, sweetheart!" Diane was home. She was smiling
at him.*

Quickly, Chuck hid the gift-wrapped package behind

him. "Oh, hi! You're home early." He stepped toward Diane. "Well, Happy Birthday!"

"Thank you," replied Diane. "By the way, whatever happened to our neighbor's wife? Did she find a doctor?"

"I really don't know."

Diane was surprised. "But, didn't you help them?"

"Well, not exactly."

"What do you mean, 'not exactly'?"

"Diane, I just never had the chance. After I hung up, I went back to the door and our neighbor was gone."

"Didn't you even try to find out what happened?"

"Well, no," answered Chuck. "I guess I got so busy eating dinner and then viewing the video on love, that I totally forgot. Which reminds me . . . " Chuck took the gift-wrapped package from behind his back and gave it to his wife. "Happy Birthday, darling!"

Diane accepted the present and began unwrapping it on the table. "I wonder what this could be?"

Inside the wrapping paper she found a large, rather ugly brown vase.

"It's . . . it's for flowers," explained Chuck. "I know how much you like flowers."

Diane looked away, the smile fading from her face.

"It was very expensive," Chuck continued, "but I got it on sale."

Diane tried unsuccessfully to hide her feelings.

"What's wrong?" asked Chuck. "Don't you like it?"

"I'm sorry Chuck." A tear began to trickle down her cheek.

"But . . . isn't it the thought that counts?"

She looked directly at Chuck. "Did you put much thought into this?"

Chuck's answer was defensive. "Uh . . . I really have been very busy."

"Chuck, my birthday comes once a year. Aren't I worth a few minutes of your time?"

All Chuck could do was nod sadly. "Well, I guess I better return this and get my money back." He picked up the large vase. Suddenly his grip on the slippery glass gave way, and despite his efforts at a mid-air recovery, it rolled off his finger tips and fell to the floor, shattering in hundreds of pieces.

Diane looked down at the remains, then at Chuck, and couldn't help laughing. Chuck smiled weakly.

In one way or another, all of us have failed at love . . . are failing at love . . . or will fail at love. Loving is the most complicated of all human skills.

And when we fail, we often make excuses:

"I didn't have the time."
"I didn't want to get involved."
"I was afraid."
"I don't know how."

Isn't it sad that the most difficult, yet the most important ability a human being can possess—to love others—is given so very little attention? We seldom spend time learning how to love. Our public schools teach nothing of the skills of love. Colleges skip over the subject. Seminaries offer no classes in loving—or helping others to love. No wonder we fail at love . . . if no one has ever taught us how, or given us a model to follow.

But there is another reason many of us don't love as well, or as often, as we should. It is because we have developed either attitudes and/or actions which interfere with our ability to love, and often cause us to fail. Our LCQ Survey provides some important insights about why we fail at love, from the over 8600 people surveyed:

■ SURVEY RESULTS

The question was asked on the LCQ Survey, "What do you feel are the barriers to love in a church?" The barriers that were mentioned, we found, could be grouped into one of two categories: either "actions" or "attitudes." The statements below are representative of the responses given:

Actions
"Remembering past bad experiences."
"Criticism of others."
"Outspoken, domineering people."

"Power struggles."
"Lack of communication."
"No time together outside the church."
"No involvement in extracurricular activities."
"Pastor not personal enough."
"Shyness of people."
"Gossip."
"People carrying grudges."
"Too busy."
"Discomfort with hugging and touching."
"Lack of follow-up to needs."

Attitudes
"Fear of change—tradition."
"Lack of close fellowship."
"People not knowing one another."
"Lack of commitment to Christ."
"Social caste system."
"Church seems too big."
"Generation gap."
"Cliques."
"Pride."
"Jealousy."
"Pettiness."
"Materialism."
"Competition."

Several months ago a friend of mine suffered a major heart attack. The paramedics had taken him to the hospital, and within only hours he had undergone a major operation to save his life. His heart was failing in its ability to perform its primary function—to circulate blood throughout the body. As the doctors told us later, it wasn't even his heart that was the original problem. It was a substance called plaque, which had accumulated on the inside of his arteries, restricting the blood flow throughout his body.

The circulation had nearly stopped because his heart could no longer do its job. The only way to save my friend's life was a major operation, a drastic dietary change, and a regular program of exercise.

Similar to the plaque that can form inside one's arteries and diminish the flow of blood through the body, there are "obstacles to love" which can easily accumulate in our lives and inhibit the flow of love through us to others. These obstacles need to be identified, confronted, and flushed out of our system.

What are these obstacles to love that keep us from loving?

We can find many of them hidden in the Apostle Paul's classic essay on love. Here he lists the qualities of love and, in the process, helps us to identify the obstacles:

Love's Ideals . . . and Love's Obstacles

Love's Ideal: "Love is patient."
Love's Obstacle: "Impatience."

Impatience describes a person whose own agenda is more important than anyone else's. He/she has little time or concern for other's concerns. An impatient person must constantly be entertained, and quickly loses interest in people if they are not filling a need in his/her own life.

The word Paul uses for "patience" describes a person who has been wronged and has the power to avenge himself, but chooses not to.[1] Impatience seeks revenge. Patience does not.

Rate yourself on the scales following each of love's obstacles.

"Most of the time, I am . . . "

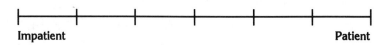

Impatient   Patient

Love's Ideal: "Love is kind."
Love's Obstacle: "Unkindness."

Some people think kindness is synonymous with weakness. Therefore, these persons reason, strength and power cannot be obtained through kindness. Those who constantly see themselves in competition with others tend to be unkind. A latent sense of inferiority is another cause for unkindness. Smedes[2] suggests that kindness is " . . . the readiness to enhance the life of another person."

"Most of the time, I am . . . "

Unkind   Kind

Love's Ideal: "Love is trusting."
Love's Obstacle: "Jealousy."

Love naturally means concern. As love grows, concern for the person also grows. But often, without one realizing it, this concern can become possessive. Jealousy is normal concern that has grown out of control, just as a cancer cell is only a normal cell grown out of control. Jealousy requires total possession—it must have exclusive rights to another person. "This emotion has the power to over-whelm and destroy the most seemingly sound and secure relationship, and the most rational person."[3]

"Most of the time, I am . . . "

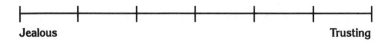

Jealous   Trusting

Love's Ideal: "Love is humble."
Love's Obstacle: "Arrogance."

Various Bible translations use different words: "boastful-ness," "rudeness," "proud," "anxious to impress," "braggart," "cherishes the idea of its own importance." Arrogant people give their "love" away as though it were a tremendous favor. Their real purpose, however, is to put others down while trying to lift themselves up.

"Most of the time, I am . . . "

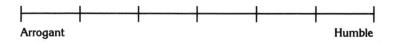

Arrogant   **Humble**

Love's Ideal: "Love is generous."
Love's Obstacle: "Selfishness."

If there is any one quality that creates an insurmountable barrier to love, it is selfishness. "Love" and "selfishness" are, by their very definition, at opposite ends of the human experience. Actions motivated by selfishness are exactly the opposite to actions motivated by love. Every selfish act takes a person that much further away from love. Christ knew about the problem of selfishness when he said, "Unless a grain of wheat falls to the ground and dies, it remains only a single seed. But if it dies, it produces many seeds."[4] Selfishness seeks its own way, and in the process loses it. Love seeks the way of others, and in the process finds its own.

"Most of the time, I am . . . "

Selfish   **Generous**

Love's Ideal: "Love is slow to anger."
Love's Obstacle: "Irritability/touchiness."

Christ had strong words for those who are quick to anger: "But now I tell you: whoever is angry with his brother will be brought before the judge; whoever calls his brother 'you good-for-nothing' will be brought before the Council; and whoever calls his brother a worthless fool will be in danger of going to the fire of hell."[5] "Wherefore, my beloved brethren," said James, "let everyman be swift to hear, slow to speak, and slow to anger."[6]

"Most of the time, I am . . . "

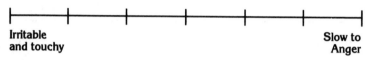

Irritable
and touchy

Slow to
Anger

Love's Ideal: "Love is forgiving."
Love's Obstacle: "Resentfulness."

Resentfulness is the accumulation of irritations suffered in the past, recalled in the present. The word Paul used for resentfulness was an accountant's word for entering an item in a ledger so it would not be forgotten.[7] This is exactly what many people do . . . and it is a great obstacle to love. "I'll forgive, but I'll never forget" mocks the true meaning of forgiveness. Resentfulness looks to the past rather than the future. The opposite of resentfulness is forgiveness. Love releases memory's grip on a wrong suffered or a hurt inflicted.

"Most of the time, I am . . . "

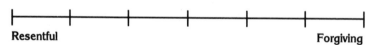

Resentful

Forgiving

Love's Ideal: "Love hates evil."
Love's Obstacle: "Loving evil."

What did Paul mean when he said, "Love hates evil?" Smedes says that loving evil is not so much finding pleasure in doing wrong, as it is the malicious satisfaction in hearing or saying something derogatory about another.[8] Surprisingly, persons who work the hardest at their high moral standards often love evil the most! As they struggle to live a life of abstinence from worldly things, they silently condemn those who do not. They gloat at the hurt or stumbling of those who "compromise with the world," and look forward to the day of judgment when these hypocrites will be cast into a lake of fire. Their message of the gospel begins with condemnation. It centers on judgment. It ends in fear. Love seems nowhere to be found.

"Most of the time, I . . . "

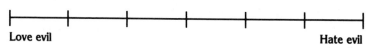

Love evil   Hate evil

Love's Ideal: "Love is always there."
Love's Obstacle: "Inconsistency."

False love has limits on its endurance. It doesn't last when things get tough. False love is like the faulty bonding of a poorly made dam that begins to lose resistance at its weakest point. A few drops of water begin to seep through the dam. The inconsistency grows to a stream, and then a torrent, and soon the entire dam gives way. Real love never fails. It is like the strong dam standing against the tremendous pressure of the water behind it. Love will bear any insult, any injury, and disappointment . . . and still be there.

"Most of the time, I am . . . "

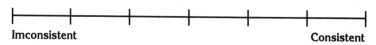

Imconsistent   Consistent

Look again at the "barriers to love" given by church members in the LCQ earlier in this chapter. Can you categorize their responses into one of these "obstacles" to love from I Corinthians? When we identify our personal obstacles to love, we have taken a step toward dealing with them as a part of our commitment to love. An effective strategy of learning to love has two parts: 1) it takes positive steps toward more intentional loving acts (outlined in Chapter Five and Six), and 2) it also identifies the obstacles to love and is constantly alert to when they begin to creep into one's life and restrict the flow of love.

For my friend who suffered a plaque-induced heart attack, the only medical solution for a healthy life was a complete change in life-style and physical behavior. Ultimately, love may also require a change in life-style and our spiritual behavior. A re-prioritizing of how we act . . . a change in the kind of spiritual nourishment we consume . . . beginning a regular program of exercise—exercise in practicing love.

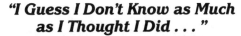

"I Guess I Don't Know as Much as I Thought I Did . . . "

That evening Chuck went for a walk and some serious thinking. His thoughtless gift had hurt Diane. "I guess I really don't know as much as I thought I did about loving," he said to himself.

Chuck recalled Diane's teasing question when she

had first learned he was going to lead the Love Seminar. "Do you really know anything about it?" she had asked.

As he walked, Chuck made a personal decision and commitment. He was going to take his preparation for the Love Seminar even more seriously, and make every effort to apply the insights himself.

Before returning home, Chuck confirmed his commitment with a brief prayer. "Lord, help me to become a more loving person. I want to make loving a priority in my life."

The Challenge . . . to Love

What about you?

What does the challenge of love . . . God's challenge of love . . . have for your life?

In this chapter we have looked at obstacles—"plaque" that builds up in the arteries of love. You have had the opportunity to rate yourself on love's ideals and love's obstacles. Can you, as a reader, make the same commitment as Chuck? Can you say, "Lord, help me to become a more loving person . . . I want to make loving a priority in my life"? If so, the coming chapters will help you put this commitment into practice.

Footnotes

1. William Barclay, *The Daily Study Bible: Letters to the Corinthians* (Philadelphia: Westminster Press, 1954), p. 133.
2. Lewis Smedes, *Love Within Limits* (Grand Rapids, MI: Eerdmans, 1978), p. 15.
3. Leo Buscaglia, *Loving Each Other* (Thorofare, NJ: Slack, Inc., 1984), p. 121.
4. John 12:24
5. Matthew 5:22
6. James 1:19
7. William Barclay, *The Daily Bible: Letters to the Corinthians* (Philadelphia: Westminster Press, 1954), p. 136.
8. Lewis Smedes, Op Cit., p. 73.

CHAPTER FOUR

The Connections of Love

*"Surely it stands to reason that only
a fuller love can compete
with the love of the world."*
H. Drummond

God loves those around us . . . *through us.*

I learned this important truth through my 2nd grade Sunday School teacher. There were ten of us in the class. One Sunday she had nine of us form a circle in the middle of the room and hold hands. She placed her Bible on a table in one corner and had the one boy who had been left out of the circle sit on a chair in the opposite corner.

She explained that the Bible on the table represented God. When one person in the circle touched God, something very special would happen to him and to everyone connected to him through their hands—it would be God's love flowing through us and on to the next person. The "game" sounded exciting.

She asked us how God's love could get into our circle if we were all in the middle of the room, while the Bible was in the corner. We concluded that our group should move over to the Bible. So, this strangely shaped circle of boys stumbled toward the table, for one of us to touch the Bible.

When we arrived, our teacher congratulated us, and we were all very proud that God's love was now flowing through our hands and around our circle.

But then she asked if, in our haste to be near God and have love flowing through our circle, we had forgotten about Matthew, the boy in the corner. We all looked at him. He seemed close to tears. We had, indeed forgotten him. Our teacher asked if we thought he was feeling God's love like the rest of us. It was obvious he wasn't. "How can we help Matthew?" she asked us.

I remember feeling sorry for him sitting in the corner without anyone to give him God's love. But none of us wanted to leave the circle to go get him . . . and lose our special connection with God. Then one boy had an idea: "One of us can stay by the Bible and we can make a line to reach over to Matt."

So, slowly we opened our circle and began to stretch. I happened to be at the front of the line and could see Matt's face brighten as we came nearer to him. He started bouncing up and down in anticipation. When I was still a few steps away, he could contain himself no longer. He leaped from the chair, shouting, "You reached me!"

I still remember how I felt—it was wonderful! I had helped Matthew touch God.

Love is being in touch with God . . . opening up and reaching out to others . . . so they, too, can touch God.

Since 33 A.D., each new generation has experienced God's love through Christians who have experienced His love, and passed it on. It is a "love delivery system" that, to this day, reaches around the world. This "delivery system" has come all the way from the first century . . . to reach you! Now you can be a part of God's "love delivery system" to those with whom you are connected.

Actually, we are not called to love anyone on our own. We are called to be "delivery systems" for God's life-changing love. We serve as channels through which people experience God's love . . . a truth reinforced by Scripture:

> "This is how we know what love is: Jesus Christ laid down his life for us. And we ought to lay down our lives for our brothers."[1]
> "Dear friends, since God so loved us, we also ought to love others."[2]
> "He has given us this command: Whoever loves God must also love his brother."[3]

To better understand this important truth—that we are God's "love connections"—consider this analogy: The San Joaquin Valley in California was, only a few generations ago, a dry and barren desert. From mid-Spring to late Fall scarcely a drop of rain falls on this 13,000 square mile area. Yet despite the regular summer drought, farms in this great valley yield more agricultural produce than any comparable area in the United States. Once a desert, the San Joaquin Valley is now a virtual "oasis."

This fruitfulness is the result of "delivery systems" which bring needed water through a large network of irrigation canals from reservoirs in the Sierra Nevada Mountains to the valley's farms and cities. These delivery systems carry water from a *source* to wherever it is needed. Without the delivery systems, the water high in the mountain reservoirs would never reach the valley below.

Consider this model as it relates to a "delivery system" channeling God's love to people. When we love someone "in Jesus' name," we are not the source of love at all. Perfect love . . . unconditional love . . . comes only from God. We are asked by God to be the channels, or delivery systems, through which His love flows . . . "because God's love has flooded our in most heart through the Holy Spirit he has given us."[4] Where there is a person whose life is a desert of loneliness, meaninglessness and hopelessness, with God's love—delivered through us—that life can become an "oasis" of joy, meaning and hope. Christ has called us to be his ambassadors[5], or delivery systems, to deliver His "living water" of love. What an awe inspiring responsibility . . . opportunity . . . challenge!

Your Connection to God. . . . the Source

Let's begin by considering our relationship with God—the Source of all love. Why? Because when we are securely connected to the Source, our life becomes an open channel through which God's love can flow. A Source-connected life, like the irrigated San Joaquin Valley, produces spiritual fruit: "love, joy, peace, patience, kindness, generosity, fidelity, adaptability, and self control . . . "[6]

In the "delivery systems" of the San Joaquin Valley, farmers know that the larger the diameter of their connecting pipes, the more water can flow to the thirsty crops. In God's "love delivery system," the analogy also holds true. The larger the "diameter" of our connection to the Source of love, the more love will flow through us to others. Some Christians have a small "diameter" of the connection linking them to God which has not been enlarged since the connection was first made (the day they came to faith). When the connection to the source is narrow, the flow of God's love through them is reduced.

How do we enlarge the "diameter of our connection," to allow more of God's love to flow through us? The Apostle Peter gives us the answer:

"Do you want more and more of God's kindness and peace? Then learn to know him better and better. For as you know him better, he will give you, through his great power, everything you need for living a truly good life."[7] Peter goes on to give a three-part strategy for the qualities that he says should be "added to your faith . . . "

1. **"Work hard to be good . . . "** Peter is saying that, in addition to our faith, we should make every effort to achieve moral excellence in our lives.

2. **"Learn to know God better . . . "** Prayer, Bible study,

Christian friends, and regular worship, can help achieve this.

3. **"Learn to put aside your own desires . . . "** The word literally means, "to take a grip on oneself." Control your desires, don't let them control you.

Spiritual growth, then, is the key to enlarging the diameter of our love connection with God. "This will make possible the next step," concludes the Apostle, "which is for you to enjoy other people and to like them, and finally you will grow to love them deeply."[8] The greater our spiritual growth, the larger the connection to the Source, and the greater the flow of love through us!

"You Call That 'Love'?"

That evening Chuck was again watching the Love Seminar video. "Some of us aren't as loving as we could be," explained the narrator, "simply because we don't know how. We have never learned the basic principles and have never developed the skills needed for building loving relationships."

Diane slipped in quietly beside Chuck and joined him in watching the video. The narrator continued, "Remember that in order for God's love to flow through you to another person, it is necessary to establish a connection, or relationship, between yourself and that person. How do you do that?"

"One basic principle is to always act first. So often in our relationships we wait for the other person to act. When it comes to initiating 'love connections,' don't wait! Always act first! And not just once. Whenever you see that other person, act first!"

Diane stopped the recorder and turned to Chuck. "You should do that with Ken."

"Do what?" asked Chuck.

"Act first."
"How do I do that?"
"I'll show you."

In the kitchen Diane had assembled a tasty plate of food. "All you have to do is go next door, ring the doorbell, and when our neighbor answers, say you heard his wife was in the hospital and you thought that he might like a home-cooked meal."

"But I don't want to do it," objected Chuck. "It's embarrassing. I'm sure I'm the last person he wants to see."

As Chuck nervously rang Ken Martin's doorbell, he asked himself why he didn't want to bring this plate of food to his neighbor? "I guess I'm just afraid," he thought to himself. "Even though I'm doing something caring, I'm not sure how he'll react. I'm not sure the rewards are worth the risks . . . and I'm sure there are risks."

The door opened and Chuck was face-to-face with his neighbor.

"Uh, hi. I'm Chuck Bradley; you know, from next

door." *Chuck shoved the foil wrapped plate at Ken.*
   "What's this?"

   "Well, it's . . . it's food," explained Chuck. "My wife heard that your wife was in the hospital and she thought you might appreciate a home-cooked meal."

   Ken pulled back a corner of the foil and inspected the contents. "Gee, thanks. That's real nice of your wife." He turned to go back inside.

   "We just want to be good neighbors," Chuck mumbled under his breath.

   "What?"

"I said . . . we want to be good neighbors. You know, like the Bible says, 'Love your neighbor'."

Ken wasn't sure he had heard correctly. "Come on. You don't love me."

"How do you know I don't?" asked Chuck.

"Well, you haven't much acted like it," replied Ken. "We've lived here for two months and you've never even said 'Hello'. You call that 'love'?"

Chuck was taken back by the candor of the conversation. "Well, I guess not," he admitted. Then after a pause, he said, "But from now on I'm gonna try!"

With that, Chuck walked away, leaving Ken slightly bewildered.

Your Connections to Others

Who are the people God wants to love . . . through you?

There are five different groups of people to whom you are God's love connection:

Family. Your family includes father, mother, spouse, children, siblings, in-laws, grandparents, grandchildren, nieces, nephews, aunts, uncles, cousins, etc. All those related to you biologically or through marriage.

Friends. These are people you enjoy being around. You invite them to dinner. You go to recreational activities together. You share yourself with them, and they with you. They're your friends.

Acquaintances. Your "acquaintances" are those with whom you are in contact on a regular basis, such as business associates, neighbors, church members, church visitors, club members, and others whom you know casually.

Enemies. In the Bible, "enemies" refers to people who initiate harmful action toward others. In Matthew 5:44, after Christ issues his well-known command to "love your enemies," He goes on to explain that enemies are a) those who speak badly of you, b) those who hate you, c) those who mistreat you, and d) those who persistently harrass you.

Needy. In both the Old and New Testaments God's people are told to show compassion to those in need.[9] Christ commanded his followers to "love your neighbor."[10] When asked who is my neighbor, Christ told the parable of the Good Samaritan as an example of a loving act to a person in need. The Apostle John also addressed this call to love those in need: "But if a man has enough to live on, and yet when he sees his brother in need shuts up his heart against him, how can it be said that divine love dwells in him?"[11] A person in need is someone in your path, perhaps in your own church, with a physical, spiritual, or emotional obstacle you can help him/her overcome. The needy are also people outside your church—people who may live right next door or on the other side of the world.

Love is doing something caring or helpful for these persons, in Jesus' name, regardless of the cost or consequences to oneself. Once we have identified the persons God wants to love through us, it becomes much easier to determine our role in the love process. Ask yourself, "how loving am I to the persons in each of these groups? . . . what have I done caring or helpful, in Jesus' name, for these persons?" Remember that you may be God's *only* love connection to some of these people.

■ SURVEY RESULTS

Question: "On a scale of 1-10, how 'loving' have you been to the following persons: spouse, parents, other family, pastor, other church members, close friends, neighbors, school/work associates?"

Notice that in Chapter One we presented survey results to a similar, but different, question from the LCQ; namely, "how *loved* do you feel from each of these people . . . ?"

How Loving are We

ON A SCALE OF
1-10 HOW LOVING
HAVE YOU BEEN
TO THE FOLLOWING
PERSONS ?

5.5	Neighbors
5.9	School & Work Associates
6.5	Church Members
6.9	Pastor
7.5	Close Friends
8.1	Family
8.2	Parents
8.7	Spouse

Looking at the relationship between love *given* and love *received* in each of the eight categories, notice that in each of the groups, members felt they *gave less* love than they received.

What a shame that most of us give less love than we receive, even though "we have learned that unexpressed love is one of the most common griefs experienced following the death of another."[12] Why wait for graveside reflections to wish we had better shared our love?

How easy or hard is it for we as Christians to say 'I love you' to these people with whom we are connected? Is it easier or more difficult for us to say it to fellow church members than to others?

■ SURVEY RESULTS

Question: "On a scale of 1-10, rate each person/s below as to how easy or hard it is for you to say 'I love you' to them, and really mean it."

We're not in the habit, even as Christians, of saying "I

love you" to many people. How many times in the last month have you said, "I love you" to your spouse; to other family members? Beyond these two groups our "comfort zone" decreases dramatically. To other relatives, it's hard. To church members and other friends, it's very difficult. Why? Is it because we really don't feel any affection toward them? Perhaps we like them, but really don't love them. Maybe it just sounds funny. In any case, they are words seldom spoken.

Yet in learning to love, we shouldn't begin with the hardest challenge—saying love—but rather with an easier challenge—showing love. Another question on the LCQ was asked, concerning how comfortable (on a scale of 1-10) did members feel about hugging and touching. There was universal consensus that this was easier than saying "I love you." And while hugging and touching is only one means of expressing love, doing loving actions is the first step toward feeling loving attitudes . . . and then finally saying loving words.

Here's a wonderful insight: with the definition of love presented in this book, we don't really need to *feel* love or even *say* love, to *do* loving acts. In fact, it happens in just the reverse. It is through *doing* loving acts that we eventually come to *feel* loving attitudes, and then to *say* loving words! It is a well-known principle of behavioral change that we must act the way we want to be. Through practicing something, we eventually become it. Through doing loving acts, we become loving persons!

■ SURVEY RESULTS

It is fascinating to study the results of this same LCQ question about saying "I love you" from the perspective of age groupings. Study the results below for the insights and implications that can be uncovered for you and your church.

Notice how it apparently becomes easier for us to say "I love you" the older we grow. With only a few exceptions, there is an increase at every age level, in every category. Young people, for example, find it extremely difficult to say "I love you" to others. In fact, it is easier for people over 66 years old to say "I love you" to "other friends" (at the bottom of their list) than it is for people under 20 years old to say those same words to their own family.

Imagine the tremendous gift we would give our young people if we could help them to better understand, express, and practice love! Could this be the missing ingredient for many churches that lack a vital, alive youth department? Could learning how to give love be a part of the purpose of your youth group, more than it is today?

Consider another issue as it relates to age and to love: is it more than a coincidence that church involvement has historically been lowest among younger people and has increased with age?[13] Plateaued or declining churches tend to have few younger people and more adults. In growing churches, it is common to see each age group well-represented and growing—a good indicator that there is love to be found in that church!

Who do we love?

There are people all around us with whom we have "love connections." Perhaps some of these people we might never have thought of in terms of love.

"Who? *Those* people? You mean my step-father? My next door neighbor? My boss? Hey, c'mon! You don't know *those* people! Maybe someone else could love them . . . maybe our pastor, or someone who doesn't know them like I do. Love my friends? . . . Well, sure, I like them; but we get along OK as it is. A comfortable distance, you know. Love my wife, my husband, my kids? . . . Of course I love them. Maybe I could show it more often, but they know I love them."

It's easy to go from day to day, moving through our own narrow "tunnels" of life and its activities, and look right past these people who are our "love connections." You are not expected to become a great lover to everyone you meet. But, there are persons in each of the categories discussed in this chapter—who need love. And whom *you can love* and be God's delivery system for His love.

New Found Riches

Here is a wonderful true story, which took place in the Rocky Mountains a little over 100 years ago. The story illustrates how we can all find treasures of love among the people around us . . .

"GOLD! GOLD!" were the shouts echoing through the hills near the town of Leadville, Colorado during the 1860's. The country was in the midst of the gold rush, and men by the thousands searched for their fortunes in the bottom of their panning tins. But sixteen years later the ruins of Leadville told of a boom town gone bust. In the nearby "California Gulch" (named after the gold dreams of the 49ers out west), only remnants of abandoned cabins and sluice boxes remained. A few diehard prospectors could still be found rewashing the gulch gravel for pocket money.

The California Gulch had a nasty reputation among the veteran prospectors. "It's that black sand!" they complained. "It gums up the riffles in sluice boxes. It fills panning holes we dug the day before. It stains and ruins clothes." The black sand seemed to cover every gold nugget with grime and grit, and make mockery of any attempt to find one's fortune. While prospectors came to Leadville in great numbers, they soon left discouraged, cursing the black sand, and moving on in search of easier streams to riches.

Into the remnants of the abandoned mines and sluice boxes of the California Gulch came two mining men, William H. Stevens and Alvinus B. Wood. Convinced there was still gold beneath the surface, they began buying up old claims. Initial gold finds heightened their efforts and expectations. But soon they, too, encountered the problems of the earlier prospectors. The black sand forced delays and hampered progress until it appeared the entire project would fall victim to the wretched grit.

One day Stevens decided to send a sample of "that black stuff" to the East coast for analysis. To their surprise, the men found the black sand was lead carbonate . . . loaded with silver!

Stevens and Wood staked lode claims throughout the California Gulch and opened the Rock Mine, the first producing silver mine in the district. They became fabulously rich in a matter of years!

The black sand . . . which miners and prospectors had cursed as an abominable intrusion in the pursuit of their golden dreams, contained wealth that would have made them rich beyond their wildest imaginations! The sandy California Gulch yielded fortunes in silver, compared to pittance in gold.

All around *you* . . . are love opportunities hidden in the "black sand." People who represent a wealth of meaningful, loving relationships. While you can cast them aside as a nuisance and intrusion into your life, you can also see them from a new perspective, and discover the hidden possibilities of love which lie buried in each of them, which hold riches in love beyond your greatest imagination!

Footnotes

1. I John 3:16
2. I John 4:11
3. I John 4:21
4. Romans 5:5
5. II Corinthians 5:20
6. Galatians 5:22 (Phillips)
7. II Peter 1:3-5 (Living Bible)
8. II Peter 1:7
9. Deut. 15:7, Psalms 41:1, Psalms 82:3, Proverbs 21:13, Matthew 19:21, Galatians 2:10
10. Matthew 19:19
11. I John 3:17
12. Leo Buscaglia, *Loving Each Other* (Thorofare, NJ: Slack Inc., 1984), p. 54.
13. Dean Hoge and David Roozen, "Research on Factors Influencing Church Commitment," *Understanding Church Growth & Decline* ed. Dean Hoge and David Roozen (New York: Pilgrim Press, 1979), p. 44-45.

CHAPTER FIVE

Getting Started Right

"To each and every one of us, love gives the promise of working miracles if we will."
Lyndia Child

Where have we come, so far, in our discoveries about love?

We have thought about the "love famine" and its ugly effects on the souls of people. We considered four foundational assumptions about love: 1) "love is the key ingredient to a fulfilled life," 2) "love can be learned," 3) "Christ wants us to love," 4) "the Source of love is God."

We have developed a working definition of love, which appears consistent with biblical understandings: *Intentionally doing something caring or helpful for another person, in Jesus' name, regardless of the cost or consequence to oneself.*

We considered why it is important to love, and found the reasons to be convincing and compelling. We looked at the reasons we often fail at love, from the perspective of Paul's great chapter in I Corinthians.

Next, we considered our "love connections," and discovered that our love is actually God's love flowing through us as we become his "delivery systems."

As we are learning about love, Chuck Bradley has been helping us translate the theory of love into reality and see the real-world application of love to life. Now as we prepare to intentionalize our love "action steps," Chuck has something to teach us about important requirements in getting off to the right start.

"No Way Am I Going to Have Anything to Do with Motorcycles!"

One afternoon when Chuck arrived home from work, he noticed his neighbor Ken tinkering with a new motorcycle. As he watched him working, Chuck asked himself, "What was that principle? . . . Act first?" Suddenly his neighbor looked up, right at him. Chuck managed an anemic wave.

Ken waved back. "Hi!"

"Oh, hi!" Chuck responded awkwardly.

"How you doin'?"

"Uh . . . I'm doing fine. Just fine," Chuck responded. "How're you doing?"

"Not too bad," answered Ken. "My wife, Chris, comes home from the hospital tomorrow."

"Hey, that's great." After a pause Chuck decided to conclude the conversation. "Well, I'll see you later."

"Yeah, see ya." Ken turned back to his motorcycle as Chuck walked to the house.

From that time on, Chuck and Ken would greet each other in a friendly manner whenever they met. However, their relationship stalled at the "Hi, how are you?" stage. Actually, Ken was friendly enough, but Chuck was afraid to get more deeply involved with someone whose life-style seemed so totally different from his. Chuck had a nagging worry that if he were to try and be more intentional at love with Ken, he might have to do some-

thing he didn't want to do . . . like get near a motorcycle. And there was no way Chuck was going to have anything to do with motorcycles!

Then there was his almost sub-conscious fear that Ken might actually respond to love, and for some reason it made Chuck slightly uncomfortable. Perhaps it was because he really didn't know what to expect as the outcome.

Chuck Bradley's approach to most "do it yourself" projects was generally unconventional. But despite his unorthodox approaches, he was usually able to "muddle through" and get the job done. Today's task was trimming the small evergreen shrub that flanked the walkway to their front door. After weeks of Diane's patient coaxing, Chuck was finally doing the job . . . albeit in a rather unorthodox manner.

Chuck had been unable to find the pruning shears. But the lack of proper tools was not about to stand in his

way. He was attacking his task—and the shrub—with a machete knife. Chuck would carefully take aim, raise the knife high above his head, and then with both hands, make a "Samurai warrior" swing at the solitary twig protruding out from the bush. And, incredible as it might seem, this strange technique seemed to work.

For Chuck, it had become more than a Saturday project. It was now an artistic enterprise. With each grandiose swing of the knife he would trim an inch or so off the shrub's foliage, then step back to study the effect and plan his next move. As he worked, Chuck envisioned himself a landscape sculptor . . . a modern-day Michelangelo, finishing another great masterpiece.

Ken Martin wasn't exactly sure what to make of this unusual scene. He approached cautiously, fearing that at any moment the imposing knife might fly from Chuck's grasp and endanger his life.

Absorbed in his work, Chuck was oblivious to the world, or the fact that Ken had come up behind him. Carefully planning his next stroke, Chuck raised the weapon over his head, forcing a quick defensive move on Ken's part. It caught Chuck's attention.

"Oh hi, Ken. How're you doing?"

"I'm doing fine. How about yourself?"

"Well, not too bad. I've almost got this licked."

"Yeah, I see that." Ken watched as Chuck continued his work. Then he posed the question that had brought him over. "Say . . . Chuck, have you ever ridden a motorcycle?"

Chuck was caught off guard. "Uh . . . no, I certainly haven't!"

"Great! That's exactly what I hoped you'd say."

Chuck was puzzled. "That's what you hoped I'd say?"

"That's right," answered Ken. "You see, I'm a writer for a motorcycle magazine, and I'm looking for someone who has never ridden a motorcycle."

Chuck breathed a sigh of relief. "Well, you've found your man."

"Good, because I've got this favor to ask you."

"Sure. What's that?"

"Well, I've got this brand new motorcycle coming," said Ken. "It's easy to ride, and I want you to test ride it for a month."

Chuck's pulse quickened. His palms became sweaty. His blood pressure rose.

"And when the month's over," continued Ken, "I'll use whatever happens as the basis for a magazine story."

Later that day Chuck was relating the incident to his

wife. "Sure," she said. "And he can title it, 'Chuck Bradley commits suicide on a motorcycle'."

"Yeah, I know." Chuck nodded. "But, Diane, what if this is the only way I can build a relationship with Ken? Maybe, like we learned in the seminar, I'm God's only 'love connection' to Ken?"

"Sweetheart, I don't want you to take the risk." Diane was very worried. "What would I do if something happened to you?"

Chuck didn't answer.

"If you love me, you won't do it."

"Diane, remember what the Apostle Paul said about becoming all things to all people?" asked Chuck. "Maybe I need to do that with Ken?"

"But Paul wasn't talking about riding motorcycles," argued Diane.

"No, he wasn't. But you have to admit Paul knew something about taking risks. Why, he risked his life to share God's love with people."

"I have been all things to all sorts of people, that by every possible means I might win some to God." [1]
—The Apostle Paul

As we purpose to become more intentional in love, there are some important prerequisites to remember . . .

1. The Right Attitude for Love—UNCONDITIONAL

A television spot produced by the Franciscan Production Center shows a Catholic Sister in the midst of a leper colony, surrounded by disease, death, and despair, caring for a group of Indian lepers. An off-screen voice comments, "I wouldn't do that for a million dollars!" The sister turns slowly to the camera and says, "neither would I."

In his book, *Unconditional Love*, John Powell says, "There is no third possibility: love is either conditional or unconditional. Either I attach conditions to my love for you, or I do not. To the extent that I do attach such conditions, I do not really love you. I am only offering an exchange, not a gift. And true love is and must always be a gift."[2]

Look again at our definition of love—*Love is intentionally doing something caring or helpful for another person, in Jesus' name, regardless of the cost or consequence to oneself.*

Did you catch the phrase? " . . . regardless of the cost or consequence to oneself." Love is unconditional. It does not need to be returned. Christ's death on the cross is the greatest illustration of the cost of love. Such love is not motivated by personal gain or reward. Real love is unselfish . . . unassuming . . . unconditional! WOW!

The importance of giving love with no expectation of return is underscored by ancient philosophers:

Plato: "Love, in its purest form, is dependent on only one of the two parties involved."

Aristotle: "Love consists in loving, rather than in being loved."

Cicero: "Thus I judge that love is to be sought, not in the hope of the reward which comes with it, but because its whole gain is in the love itself."

Scripture reinforces this attitude of giving love, even when love is not received: " . . . but Christ died for us while we were yet sinners, and that is God's own proof of His love toward us."[3] Or, again, "Let this mind [attitude] be in you which was also in Christ Jesus, who though He was God, did not cling to his rights as God, but laid aside His mighty power and glory, taking upon himself the form of a servant."[4]

What an important truth to learn—that love's great reward is in the giving, rather than in the receiving. Recognize and act on this truth, and you have the right attitude for love—unconditional.

2. The Right Foundation for Success— COMMITMENT

"If I Hadn't Gotten the Brake and Clutch Mixed Up . . . "

Ken had chosen a vacant parking lot as the location for Chuck's first lesson. Chuck sat nervously on the small motorcycle, trying to appear calm, as Ken helped him put on a helmet.

"Come on, Chuck, just relax and enjoy it. There's really nothing to worry about."

With Ken's help Chuck found the kick start and started the engine. He then timidly engaged the gear, released the clutch, and was off on his first jerky, terrify-

ing motorcycle ride around the parking lot. Chuck's control was minimal and his balance saved only by his feet serving as "training wheels" on either side of the bike. The cycle seemed to have a mind of its own. Chuck wobbled around in something approximating figure eights, narrowly missing Ken each time around.

Ken shouted out encouragement. "Keep your feet up. Try a larger circle."

"What?" yelled Chuck, looking in Ken's direction.

"Look out," screamed Ken. "Watch where you're going!"

Chuck looked back just in time to see the edge of the parking lot and the steep drop-off just beyond.

Ken watched helplessly as his pupil rode the new motorcycle down the bank and out of sight . . .

Diane was gently cleaning Chuck's bruised and bleeding elbow. "Sweetheart, I hope you've learned your lesson. You could have been killed."

Chuck winced, looking at the bruises and cuts he had just acquired. "I'd have been all right if I hadn't gotten the brake and the clutch controls mixed up."

Diane reached for another bandaid. "Well, thank God you won't be doing anything like this again."

"Oh, I'm not giving up on Ken."

"But you certainly don't intend to do any more motorcycle riding, do you?" asked Diane.

"If I want to build a relationship with Ken, I may have to."

"But what about me? Don't you care how I feel?"

"Of course I care how you feel," replied Chuck.

"Then, if you love me, you'll give up this motorcycle business."

Chuck winced again as Diane applied antiseptic to one of his several facial cuts. "Are you using love to manipulate me?"

"Is that what you think?" She stopped and looked directly at Chuck. "That I'm manipulating you?"

"Diane, instead of worrying about me and feeling

sorry for yourself, why don't you try getting acquainted with Ken's wife, Chris?"

The right foundation for success in loving is *commitment*.

Now, it's not always necessary to risk your life on a motorcycle in order to love your neighbor. However, genuine love means becoming involved in the lives of other people. It means entering into their world, and often doing things that are new and different. Building a "love connection," in which God's love can flow through you to another person, will likely be costly in terms of time, effort, and risk.

After his inspired comments on love to the church in Corinth, Paul encouraged the new believers to make a commitment to love: "let love be your greatest aim."[5] To the believers in Colossae he called for a commitment to love: "Above everything else, be truly loving, for love is the golden chain of all the virtues."[6] Peter, too, echoes the high priority required for love: "Above all, love each other deeply . . . "[7] A commitment to love is clearly called for by the Master, himself: "A new commandment I give to you: Love one another. As I have loved you, so you must love one another. All men will know you are my disciples if you love one another."[8]

Did you realize that in the New Testament the call to love appears more frequently than any other imperative? Can any serious Christian ignore this call? A *commitment* to love is a foundation for success.

3. The Right Approach to People—ACCEPTANCE
The ideal: to be completely accepting of others . . . to see them as God sees them. They are created in His image—they have dignity and worth. They need to be loved, just as we need to be loved.

. . . **but, the reality:** It's hard!

I must confess, I'm not as genuinely accepting of people as I would like to be. It's easy to be critical of others . . . to look for faults . . . to silently smile at the failures of those around us. To be genuinely accepting of people is easier said than done. When I discuss this problem with other Christians, I find I am not alone. Many of us tend to be less accepting of those whose life-styles, values, or attitudes are different than our own.

Why do we struggle in this area? Why aren't we more accepting? Why should we, as persons connected to the Source of love, have difficulty with acceptance and forgiveness? Have we forgotten that, through Jesus Christ, we are accepted and forgiven by God Himself?

As I think about my own need to be more accepting of people, I can see where my past had an influence on my view of people.

I grew up with a number of misunderstandings about God's acceptance and forgiveness. While I understood that God loved me, I also understood that God was holy, righteous, and just. Obviously such a God could not accept me if, and when, I sinned. As a child, I lived each day in fear that I would die before I had asked Almighty God to forgive my latest sin.

Even though I had a personal relationship with Jesus Christ, I was constantly unsure whether God really loved me the way I was. Each Sunday night at church, we were asked by the pastor or a guest evangelist to re-examine our lives and find those personal sins for which we needed repentance. And almost every Sunday night I came forward to repent. I did a lot of repenting, but very little growing. Though I had committed my life to Christ, I lived in constant fear of the wrath of God.

Today, I know that God's love and acceptance of me is unconditional. But for years I honestly believed that God would accept me only after I had uttered my plea of forgiveness. It wasn't until my mid-thirties that I finally realized my perception of God was extremely wrong.

Another factor in my upbringing affected my acceptance of people.

My Christian parents were constantly judging other people's life-styles on the basis of which "don'ts" they "did." I, too, became highly critical of people's life-styles—whether they smoked, drank, danced, played cards, wore makeup, or went to movies. If someone were guilty of any of the above, I mentally condemned them. If they claimed to be "Christians," I seriously questioned their faith.

This is not to say high moral standards are unimportant. They are. But a preoccupation with the outward aspects of a person's life-style can make it nearly impossible to accept people who are different from us.

Parents are so important in shaping attitudes of acceptance in children. A close friend of my oldest son grew up believing his parents would only accept and love him if he did his very best. For most of his life Bob did only those things which would make his parents proud. His high school experience culminated in being selected valedictorian and keynote student speaker at graduation. But college was more difficult than Bob expected. His first year in pre-med was extremely competitive. His grades went down. He got involved in drugs. His perfect world unravelled.

Unable to face his parents, Bob took his own life. He thought his parents' acceptance was conditional. In a note to his parents, he said, "Mom and Dad, I'm sorry to have let you down." Bob had failed to meet what he perceived to be the conditions for his acceptance, and he believed that his parents would no longer love him.

The Right Model

What a model for acceptance we have in Jesus Christ!
The Pharisees were continually critical of him for asso-

ciating with and accepting "publicans and sinners." There was Mary Magdalene, who had a most dubious past. Yet Jesus accepted her and extended his love to her. There was Matthew, a hated tax collector. Yet Jesus not only accepted him, but chose him as a disciple. On the cross, Jesus extended acceptance and love to the thief who hung with him. He even extended forgiveness to those who were crucifying him: "Father, forgive them, for they do not know what they are doing."[9]

Remember that God's love and acceptance can transform any life. The right approach to love is being willing to accept others . . . as He accepts you.

"Apparently Loving and Motorcycling Had Something in Common."

Chuck did not give up on Ken. And although in the beginning it was pretty scary, he stuck with motorcycling. He returned with Ken to the empty parking lot and accepted the challenge of conquering his fear and learning the basic riding techniques. For most of an entire Sunday afternoon, he rode slow "figure eights" and other training routines until his teacher felt he was ready for the street.

Chuck discovered that it took a lot of time and practice to learn the skills of motorcycle riding, but he also found that the more he learned, the less afraid he became. There was something invigorating about experiencing the out-of-doors on a motorcycle. Travelling back country roads with Ken was an experience Chuck had never known. It was fun!

In the process, Chuck became much better acquainted with his cycling neighbor. At first, he had found it nearly as scary relating to Ken on a deeper personal level, as it had been learning to ride a motorcycle.

As time went on, Chuck began to feel more comfortable with Ken and found he was enjoying the relationship, as well as the motorcycling. Apparently, loving and motorcycling had something in common—the more you practiced, the more you reduced your fear, and the more you enjoyed it.

However, Diane didn't enjoy those days nearly as much as Chuck did. She would spend her time pacing nervously, frequently glancing at the clock and then out the window. Each time Chuck returned safely, Diane would have to ask herself if her fears were groundless. "Was Chuck right? Was this something he had to do?" And for some reason, it bothered her that Chuck seemed to enjoy spending so much time with Ken and this new found hobby.

As Chuck's relationship with Ken grew, he thought back about the earlier days, and wondered, "How many times have I assumed a person was someone I couldn't relate to? And because of that, I kept my distance and wrote that person off?" Chuck realized it had happened *more than once, and that he had been wrong to make assumptions about people before getting to know them. He had to admit that he had been very wrong about Ken.*

Frequently, as Chuck and Ken were riding together, other bikers would give friendly waves as they passed. At rest stops Chuck experienced a warm camaraderie with many of these riders. They would share travel information, discuss the new models of motorcycles, and accept newcomers like Chuck as if they were old friends. More than once Chuck found himself comparing this amiable fellowship to his church, and wondering whether these cyclists weren't often friendlier to strangers than some church members.

Chuck realized that if he was going to be God's "love connection" to people outside the church, it meant learning to accept these people, following the example of Christ, who was a friend to publicans and sinners. "I guess I've been in the church so long," he once commented to Diane, "that the only people I felt comfortable around were other Christians. But if I only love other Christians, how will non-Christians ever experience God's love?"

The Right Strategy for Change

For many of us, our sincere Sunday morning resolutions about love begin slipping into the sub-conscious somewhere around Monday afternoon. The deadline at work is missed . . . the kids are screaming . . . the car overheats on the freeway! Oh, for the peace and tranquility of the Sunday morning service!

Is it realistic to try and prioritize our life around love? Can we *really* change? Can we, as mere humans, attain this Godly ideal? Can we learn love attitudes . . . and then put them into practice?

I had very good reasons for improving my fitness and nutrition. For one, my waistline was beginning to extend beyond acceptable limits. I was so out of shape that even walking the dog had become tiring. My father and grandfather had both died prematurely of cardiovascular disease. I had been told that anyone with my genetic heredity should be active in a regular exercise program.

But I just couldn't do it! Time after time I had enthusiastically begun an exercise program, only to drop out within a few weeks. My favorite Scripture verse had become, "the spirit is willing, but the flesh is weak."

However, three years ago, I began an exercise program . . . and to this day I am still with it! Why did I succeed this time after failing on every previous effort? The difference was that I found a *workable strategy for personal change.*

In contrast to my previous efforts, I began my current exercise program slowly, with expectations that were realistic . . . for me. I rode a stationary bicycle for only two minutes every day, three days a week. To prevent boredom, I read interesting books as I pedaled. Gradually I increased the time from two minutes, to three, and more. Finally, after three months, I was able to ride continuously for thirty minutes without "running out of gas."

Then I bought and began riding a ten-speed bicycle. When the weather was good I would ride the 20-minute bicycle trip to work three times a week and rest on the weekends. As the weeks went by, my strength and skill increased. I began taking weekend rides.

My progress toward improved fitness has been slow, but steady. Regular exercise has affected my eating habits. My metabolism now functions at a rate comparable to when I was in my teens. I have shed unwanted pounds and my waist has returned to its previous size. My pulse has decreased from 73 to 50. I feel good. And I now *enjoy* the conditioning process. I look forward to my bike rides. It's an important part of my life.

What does this have to do with loving people "in Jesus' name"? I believe the principles which helped me in health and fitness apply to improving our ability to love. The need is simply to adopt a workable strategy for change. What are the key elements?

A. Begin Slowly with Realistic Expectations.

Have realistic expectations . . . of yourself. Otherwise, you are setting yourself up for failure. For example, if you are shy, don't begin by forcing yourself to initiate relationships with strangers. You can grow into that later. Instead, begin by trying to improve the quality of your relationships.

If verbal conversation is not your strength, don't begin marathon talks with people you are just learning to know. Instead, concentrate on being a good listener. While you might prepare yourself in advance by planning some questions or topics for dialogue, be satisfied with just a few minutes of conversation.

When you take the specific steps of love (presented in the next chapter), *begin slowly with realistic expectations of yourself.* As a result you will be successful in starting a process to ultimately reach your love potential.

B. Be Consistent.

In the fitness area, this means following a strict (yet realistic) schedule. One doesn't improve his/her fitness level by working out one week, then skipping two. The same is true in improving our ability to love. It's not an "on again, off again" process. Be regular and consistent.

As in fitness, it's not only all right to begin at a slower pace, it's recommended. But the slower pace must be repeated *consistently.* It's the same when it comes to loving. We only improve our skills when we use them regularly. The intensity and duration of our initial love efforts can be minimal, provided they are frequent.

If time is a problem, again begin slowly. But *be consis-*

tent. A few minutes spent relating to another person is far better than spending no time at all; or even a large amount of time only once.

When you are consistent at your efforts to love, you will find that your abilities and capabilities increase. And you will begin to enjoy it!

C. Learn All You Can.

The more I learned about fitness, the easier it was to make progress. Not only are mistakes avoided, but the learning itself becomes an enjoyable part of the fitness process. I became an avid reader of bicycling magazines, read books on nutrition and conditioning, and purchased dozens of paperback books on related subjects. As time went on, I found that my pleasure reading was almost entirely on this subject. The result of this learning was that my skills developed and my commitment level increased.

The same thing happens in improving our love-ability. The way to guarantee success in loving is to keep learning about it. Study on your own. There are many helpful books by both Christian and secular writers. Of course, studying the Scriptural insights on love is important. Study with others. Attend classes or seminars at your church on loving and related subjects.[10] If there are none, talk to leaders in your church and plan such classes. Use this book as a text for class.

Your study will be considerably more helpful if, in the process, you are *practicing* steps to initiate and build loving relationships "in Jesus' name." Remember, learning to love is a "lab class," not a "lecture class." As you gain experience in loving others, you will have questions and problems which need answers. Finding these answers together in a supportive group will help your study program work.

Learning—by itself—will never improve one's physical fitness. There is no substitute for exercise. However, learning, combined with exercise, not only makes an exercise program more effective, but it also heightens the interest and increases the enjoyment. Similarly, just learning about love will never improve our ability to love other people. But learning, when combined with practical exercises in caring and relating to others, is a key to guaranteeing success in love.

D. Enjoy the Process.

I enjoy bicycling. That's one reason I've been successful with my current exercise program. I like it! That doesn't mean I smile continuously while struggling to the top of a steep hill. But I do smile when I reach the top and antici- pate the cool wind blowing in my face as I reap the rewards of my efforts.

Any process of change involves pain and struggle. There will always be hills. Yet the process must be essen- tially satisfying and enjoyable, or we won't stick it out. At the same time, whether cycling or loving, the more we do it, the better we become. And the better we become, the more we enjoy it!

Love will require effort on your part, and not every situ- ation will leave you smiling. There will be some tired mus- cles, some sweat, perhaps a skinned knee when you fall, or bruised ego when others see you fall. But being partners with God—in loving other people—will become so satis- fying and enjoyable that when you do make it to the top, and feel the cool breeze blowing in your face, you will won- der why you waited so long.

How about getting in shape—to love!

Footnotes

1. I Corinthians 9:22
2. John Powell, *Unconditional Love* (Allen, TX: Argus Publishers, 1978), p. 65.
3. Romans 5:8
4. Philippians 2:5-7
5. I Corinthians 14:1 (Living Bible)
6. Colossians 3:14 (Phillips)
7. I Peter 4:8
8. John 13:34-35
9. Luke 23:34
10. A helpful study course based on the book *Who Cares About Love?* has been produced by Church Growth, Inc. (1921 S. Myrtle Ave., Monrovia, CA 91016). The course is called *Growing in Love* and includes a video tape which follows the story line of Chuck Bradley presented in this book. A free brochure is available upon request.

CHAPTER SIX

Steps to Loving

"Most of us long for stronger, more creative, and rewarding ways of loving each other."
Leo Buscaglia

Is there love without action? No.

We experience love only when someone else *gives* love. How is love given? Through action.

How, then, do we put love into action?

"Any enterprise is built by wise planning, becomes strong through common sense, and profits wonderfully by keeping abreast of the facts."[1] This biblical proverb is particularly useful as we design our approach to intentionally loving the selected people in our "love connections." Being God's love channel requires our best planning.

The eight steps presented in this chapter will help you put love into action. By seriously following these steps, the benefits to you and to others will be great. Because to love, in Jesus' name, regardless of the cost or consequence to oneself . . . will be the most important thing you have ever done.

STEP ONE   Make a "Love Covenant" with God

Without serious commitment, none of the principles or steps of love proposed in this book will work. Loving is a life-style, not an on-again, off-again activity. A "love-covenant" is your personal statement to God of your desire for renewal and rededication to what He calls you to do and to be. When you make a "love-covenant" with God you are telling Him that you are personally willing, as the Apostle Paul said, "to make love your aim."[2]

A "love-covenant" with God should have the same faithful intent that God has in His covenant promises to us: "Though the mountains be shaken, and the hills be removed, yet my unfailing love for you will not be shaken nor my covenant of peace be removed."[3]

You might find it helpful to write out your love-covenant with God. It is your request for His help and strength in fulfilling this new priority in your life—love.

STEP TWO   Identify Those Who Specifically Need Your Love

You may have made a list of people in your "love connections," from Chapter Four. If so, this is the time to review it, looking for any additions or omissions. If you have not made a specific list, do it now. Refer to page 59 and begin identifying the people in your love connections. In making your list be sure to include both Christians and non-Christians.

Remember, we are delivery systems for God's love to others—family, friends, associates, enemies, and those in need. These are the people God is waiting to "deliver" his love to . . . through you.

In making your "connection" list, start with your family.

Then, list your close friends: people you enjoy being with, those you would invite over for dinner, or enjoy going out with to a special event.

Next on your connection list are acquaintances: people

at work or school, in your neighborhood, in your recreational or social relationships.

The list now becomes more challenging, as you identify your enemies. According to the definition in Chapter Four, these may be church members or non-members.

Finally, think about any persons who may not be in one of the above categories, but who have a specific need to which you can respond.

Of course, there are differences between the people in these five groups, how we relate to them, and what it means to love them. The closer these connections are to us (such as families and close friends), the more permanent are our relationships. The more distant the connections, such as casual acquaintances, enemies, and perhaps certain needy persons, the less permanent are the relationships. Remember our definition of love: *Intentionally doing something caring or helpful for another person, in Jesus' name, regardless of the cost or consequence to oneself.* This definition provides opportunities for loving the people in each of these groups, regardless of how permanent or passing the relationship may be.

Review the names on your list. Select one or two people from each of the five categories (family, friends, acquaintances, enemies, needy) with whom you can begin to practice "love actions" in the coming days and months. In selecting the people you intend to focus attention on, consider your capacity to love, your time available, and your own commitment to love. Loving another person takes time and effort. Be realistic about your ability and availability.

STEP THREE Act First
Remember that this was one of Chuck Bradley's early lessons as he grew in love. Don't wait for the other person. Always act as though the responsibility for the initiation and growth of that loving relationship depends entirely on

you. This holds true for strengthening old love relationships, as well as establishing new love relationships.

Often we wait for the other person to make the first move. Will he stop? Will she smile? Will he speak first? Will she call or invite me over? When it comes to intentional love . . . *always* act first! And not just once, but again and again . . . whatever is necessary to make the relationship come "alive." Make a life-style of acting first!

STEP FOUR   Communicate

Research indicates that people believe the most important ingredient for loving relationships is communication.[4]

As communication grows, love grows. There are various levels of communication in which we interact. In a sense, these levels are communication "stepping stones" to new understanding. They cannot be by-passed or ignored. As you begin to intentionally love the people you have identified, ask yourself, "on what level do I communicate (if at all) with each person?"

The first level of communication is the exchange of cliches. "Hi, how are you?" And whether we feel like it or not, our response is "Fine, how are you?" At this level, we don't do much except share cliches. "So, have a nice day . . . " "You, too."

The second level of communication shares data and information. Talk is about things which are impersonal and non-threatening—the weather, the ball game, the job, a television program, world events. "Looks like rain."

The third level is when we begin to share something about who we are—our opinions and attitudes, our dreams, goals, and values. This level begins the sharing of ourself with another. "Here is what's really important to me . . . "

The fourth, and most intimate level of communication, is when we share our feelings, emotions, joys, and fears with another person. There is a difference between opinions (the third level) and feelings (the fourth level). "I feel we should do this . . . " is an opinion. "I feel anxious about this . . . " is a feeling. Intimacy comes in sharing openly with another person. This level of communication requires a well-developed level of mutual trust.[5] "I do love you . . . "

Sometimes we communicate very well when first beginning a loving relationship . . . when we are at the first or second level. But we can easily stagnate at one of these levels. Try moving up from your present level to the next. Go beyond cliches. Talk about more than the daily news or the weather. Stretch yourself beyond intellectual ideas. Take a tentative step toward sharing your feelings. Admit some of your fears, your hurts, your frustrations, your disappointments . . . and share your joys!

A sociologist recently conducted a survey to find out how much time family members spend in meaningful communication. At the low end of the scale, he found that the average American father spends only six minutes a week really communicating with his teenage daughter. At the high end, he found that the average husband and wife spend 29 minutes a week in meaningful dialogue.[6]

Studies indicate that men have particular trouble in sharing themselves. A recent study found that 75% of the women interviewed could, without hesitation, name at least one intimate friend. More than 66% of the men could not.[7] Traditionally our society teaches males to hide or overcome their feelings. Leading psychologists estimate that only 10% of the adult males in the United States have anyone with whom they can intimately relate.[8] The step of "sharing yourself" is indeed a challenge.

How do we improve our communication? Here are three simple suggestions:

• **Active listening.** "Be quick to hear," says James.[9] "An open ear is the only believable sign of an open heart."[10] A prominent theologian said, "The first duty of love is to listen."[11] We are all born with the capacity to hear; but the ability to listen must be deliberately cultivated. Good listening requires concentration. It involves eye contact and body language. It means focusing exclusively on what the other person is trying to communicate.

• **Remembering.** If you have trouble remembering, make notes after you've been together. If something is mentioned in conversation, write it down and do something about it—perhaps an idea for a gift that shows you were listening and you care. Remembering is particularly important when *initiating* love actions to persons with whom you have a less intimate relationship (acquaintances, enemies, those in need). A technique like this may sound unnecessary, but it works. Try it.

• **Honesty.** Make an intentional effort to be forthright and open. McGinnis calls it "cultivating transparency."[12] Clearing the air can often help a relationship grow. However, love also means there are things better left unsaid. Honesty and tact are *both* part of loving communication.

There are many excellent books on communication. If this is an area in which you feel the need for growth, study and learn more about the dynamics of good communication.

STEP FIVE   Empathize

The morning paper recently featured a moving example of loving empathy. It was a story about a young man with cancer, and of his friends and family who tried to say they cared. Here is part of the article:

Manuel Garcia feared that when he shaved his head to get rid of the patches of hair left by chemotherapy, "I would feel very self-conscious that everyone would stare at me."

He didn't need to worry.

Before Garcia was released from the Milwaukee Medical Complex after treatment, his friend and three relatives came into his room with bald heads. "I woke up, and just started laughing," said Garcia. "Then they told me, 'We're here so you won't be alone.'

When he arrived home his house and neighborhood were teeming with bald heads—all in the name of love for Manuel Garcia, in his fight against cancer. "My oldest boy had beautiful hair," said Garcia of his son who had wanted his head shaved. "Last night he said, 'Daddy, I did it because I love you.'"

"I cut my hair because I've known him for 15 years and I love him like a father," said Dale Wetzel, 26. "It helped me to understand how he felt; it made me feel good inside."

When Garcia had been diagnosed as having cancer, he was extremely depressed. "But I'm ready for anything now," he says. "I feel 100% better."[13]

Empathy means "identification with, or vicariously experiencing the thoughts, feelings, or attitudes of another person."[14] In a sense, you become that person. You see the world through their eyes. You experience what they experience . . . you feel the way they feel.

STEP SIX   Identify a Love Opportunity

Is there a hurt or an opportunity where your love can help? Jesus spoke of love that responds to needs:

> "For I was hungry and you fed me; I was thirsty and you gave me water; I was a stranger and you invited me into your home; naked and you clothed me; sick and in prison, and you visited me. Then these righteous ones will reply, 'Sir, when did we ever see you hungry and feed you? Or thirsty and give you anything to drink? Or a stranger and help you? Or naked, and clothe you? When did we ever see you sick or in prison, and visit you?' And I, the King, will tell them, 'When you did it to these my brothers, you were doing it to me.'"[15]

The love opportunity may be a physical need. It may be

an emotional need; a relational need; or a spiritual need.

Everyone has needs. As you spend time with a person, through good communication and empathy, you will discover opportunities for loving actions. Then, you can take the next step . . .

STEP SEVEN   Respond with a Caring Gift

A well thought-out gift is a unique expression of love. Look at the greatest giver and gift of all . . . God and His Son.

A gift should be *meaningful* . . . based on the needs of the person receiving it.

A gift should be *sacrificial* . . . or it is just a convenience.

A gift should be *unexpected* . . . rather than predictable, due to protocol or expectation.

A gift should be *motivated by love* . . . unconditionally, with no expectation of return.

Gifts are not always purchased at the local shopping mall. You might give the gift of forgiveness to a person who is in need of it; there is the gift of appreciation to a person who feels neglected; there is the gift of support to a person who feels alone and uncertain. Whatever the need, yours may be the gift that is needed most.

STEP EIGHT   Share Yourself

Sharing your most treasured possession is hard to do, because it's all you have . . . it is you. The ultimate step of love is to give yourself to another. Wedding vows between a new husband and wife are perhaps the most visible form of this commitment to love. Unfortunately, as we have seen in our LCQ survey , such genuine, shared love is most often limited to spouse and immediate family.

But sharing yourself need not be limited to one person, or one family.

Sharing yourself is when love-actions become a way of life to those persons in your love connections. Sharing yourself is loving another person as yourself.

In a sense, "sharing yourself" isn't really an eighth step to take, as much as it is a result of having taken the first seven steps enough times with enough people to where you actually *become* a loving person. You are Ebenezer Scrooge . . . on Christmas morning! You have discovered that love really is the answer, when it is shared . . . through sharing yourself.

For each person it will be different. It means more than a one-time gift. Sharing yourself is far more of a sacrifice. It means giving all that you are. It goes to the very essence of who you are and what you hold dear. It is imitating the love modeled by Christ. It is striving toward the kind of love Christ asks from us when we follow Him: "Be ye perfect, even as my Father in heaven is perfect."[16]

Sharing yourself is what the Apostle John described as "laying down your life for your brother."[17] Jesus spoke of this ultimate goal as to "love your neighbor as yourself."[18] Of course, he demonstrated that love when he gave his own life.

It is easier to move on to this ultimate step of sharing yourself if we remember that we are really just channels for *God's love* to the people in our "love connections." Through our love, others begin to experience the person and power of that perfect love.

Put Love into Action

In the final analysis, love is nothing until it becomes action.

Just about everyone knows the Jim Brady story—how the big, bluff, quick-witted "Bear," only two months after becoming White House press secretary, was shot in the head during the attempted assassination of President Reagan; and how he has fought his way back from brain surgery and the crippling, enduring damage from the stray bullet.

Not many people know, however, about the ceaseless, selfless, singleminded, devoted love of Bob Dahlgren . . . a man who loved Brady like himself.

A few months ago Bob Dahlgren died in his sleep, at 52 years of age. It didn't even make the morning news. But during the long months following the shooting, it was Dahlgren who took the vigil with Brady's wife Sarah, through the long series of brain operations. It was Dahlgren and his wife Suzie, who took the Bradys' young son Scott into their home through the early days of the ordeal.

It was Dahlgren who helped ease the way toward recovery by arranging convivial "happy hours" with Brady's friends by his hospital bedside.

As Brady recovered and was able, in a wheelchair, to return to a semi-normal life, it was Dahlgren, always Dahlgren, who scouted out the advance arrangements, who helped load and unload his friend from the specially equipped van in which Brady did most of his traveling.

It was Dahlgren who helped Sarah field the interminable questions about Brady's health and who spent endless hours keeping Brady's friends posted on his condition, who dealt with the doctors, lawyers, exploiters, bandwagon-climbers.

It was Dahlgren who helped organize a foundation to assure financial support for the family.

For more than $4\frac{1}{2}$ years after Brady was shot, Bob Dahlgren devoted virtually all his time to the man he loved. And he did so with little recognition, and no hint of seeing anything in return. Never, ever did Dahlgren complain. Never did he hesitate when needed. Never did he stop looking for the needs or the response of love.

As Dr. Arthur Kobrine, the surgeon who lived through Brady's long ordeal with him, once said, "everyone should have a friend like Bob Dahlgren."[19]

"Love is not a matter of words or talk, it must be genuine and show itself in action."[20]

You've heard the phrase, "It's the thought that counts"? Do you know what? It's *not* the thought that counts . . . it's the *action* that counts. As you begin to implement these eight steps to better loving, remember the guidelines from Chapter Five for getting in shape to love: a) begin slowly with realistic expectations, b) be consistent, c) learn all you can, and d) enjoy the process. Through these simple, yet important steps, you can put love into action! In so doing, your love habits will begin to change . . . and you will experience the exciting process of sharing God's love— through your life and your love—with the people around you.

"Your Church Really Takes This Love Thing Seriously"

The night air was crisp with the onset of autumn. Ken, holding a manuscript in one hand, rang the doorbell of the Bradley house and then leaned wearily against the wall to wait. He felt tired. The all-night writing sessions seemed to be getting harder and harder.

The door opened and Chuck greeted him. "Hi, Ken. Won't you come in?"

Ken straightened up. "No thanks. I've got to get home and get some sleep."

"You do look tired. You OK?"

"Yeah. I've just been up all night finishing my article." Ken handed the manuscript to Chuck. "I wanted you to have a chance to read it before it gets published."

"Well, thanks," said Chuck. "How soon do you need this back?"

"I don't. That's your copy." Ken hesitated before adding. "I hope you like it . . . especially the ending."

"Oh, I'm sure I will." Chuck looked at Ken with concern. "Ken, be sure you get that sleep."

"I will, Chuck. Good night."

"Good night."

———————

"So, that's what happened when I helped a non-rider discover motorcycling." Diane was reading Ken's article aloud to Chuck. "The best part of the whole experience for me was that I found a real friend. Chuck is fun to be with. He accepts me the way I am and really seems to care about me. He talks to me. But more important, he listens . . . and he hears." Diane smiled as she continued. "Chuck has given me a new understanding of what a real friend is. In fact, from now on, my personal definition of a friend will be—Chuck Bradley."

"Sweetheart, that's beautiful!" Diane put down the article and looked at him. "Chuck, I'm sorry I acted so selfishly. I was wrong. It was a risk you had to take."

"And I think you are also wrong putting off getting acquainted with Chris."

Diane looked down for a moment and then began slowly nodding her head. *"You're right."*

"No more excuses?" asked Chuck.

"No more excuses. I'll call her right now!" Diane got up and went to the phone.

As Diane was introducing herself to Chris on the phone, Chuck reflected on what had happened in the past few months. He realized that Ken's story would have had a much different ending if he hadn't followed the principles of love he had been learning at church: *"Always Act First;" "Communicate;" "Empathize;" "Identify a Love Opportunity;"* and the rest of the principles of love. As he looked back on the experience, he could honestly say that he had really enjoyed the process. It had helped him break out of his old and often unloving habits. He felt that, while Ken had obviously benefited, he, too, could say that the love given really did return many times over in his own personal life and growth.

Chuck had been preparing for the final Love Seminar when Ken dropped in.

"I hope you don't mind my barging in like this, but I just had to get away from my typewriter. I can only stare at a blank page for so long."

"Don't mind at all. Sit down."

"Thanks."

Chuck took a good look at his friend. "Are you okay? You still look tired."

"Oh, I'm having trouble sleeping," said Ken. "Other than that, I'm fine." Ken changed the subject. "How're you doing?"

"Oh, I'm doing fine. I'm just preparing for the final session of a so-called 'Love Seminar' which I'm leading at our church."

"Your church really takes this love thing seriously."

"Well, we're trying to," said Chuck.

"I guess I always thought the only thing churches took seriously was raising money," continued Ken. "Chris and I haven't done much church-going, but if everyone in your church is like you and Diane . . . well, we might be interested."

Chuck smiled.

"By the way, did you get a chance to read my article?" asked Ken.

"Yeah . . . I did."

"What did you think?"

"Well," Chuck was a little uncertain about what to say. "It was very well written . . . but to be honest, the ending was . . . well . . . it was sort of embarrassing. I don't think I'm that great a friend."

"But, Chuck, you are," insisted Ken. "And that article was my way of thanking you for being such a good friend."

Footnotes

1. Proverbs 24:3-4 (Living Bible)
2. I Corinthians 14:1
3. Isaiah 54:10
4. Leo Buscaglia, *Loving One Another* (Thorofare, NJ: Slack, Inc., 1984), p. 36.
5. Dick Day, from the film "Maximum Dating," produced by Johnson-Nyquist Film Productions. Presented in a lecture on July 3, 1985 in Mission Viejo, CA.
6. Flavil Yeakley, in *The Quest for Growth* (unpublished manuscript), p. 5.
7. Lillian Rubin. *Just Friends: The Role of Friendship in Our Lives* (New York: Harper & Row, 1985).
8. Paul Robbins, "Must Man Be Friendless," in LEADERSHIP, Fall, 1984, p. 25.
9. James 1:19
10. David Augsburger, *Caring Enough to Hear and Be Heard* (Ventura, CA: Regal Books, 1982), p. 149-150.
11. Paul Tillich, In *The Friendship Factor,* by Alan Loy McGinnis (Minneapolis: Augsburg Publishing House, 1979), p. 109.
12. Alan Loy McGinnis, *The Friendship Factor* (Minneapolis: Augsburg Publishing House, 1979).
13. Pasadena Star News, July 20, 1985, p. B8.
14. The Random House Dictionary of the English Language, (New York: Random House, 1968), p. 433.
15. Matthew 25:35-40
16. Matthew 5:48
17. I John 3:16
18. Mark 12:33
19. Raymond Coffey, "He was Jim Brady's best friend" in PASADENA STAR-NEWS, November 3, 1985, p. A-5.
20. I John 3:18

CHAPTER SEVEN

"Who Cares About Love? . . . I Do!"

*"Love spoken can be turned aside.
Love demonstrated is irresistable."*
Stanley Mooneyham

Chuck was enjoying his hard work. The early Spring sunshine was pleasant and warm, and the air was freshened by a gentle breeze. It was one of those days it just felt good to be alive.

As he worked, Chuck reflected on the months that had elapsed since the completion of Ken's article. During that time he and Diane had become close friends with both Ken and his wife, Chris. The Love Seminar, which Chuck led, had met with genuine success and the church was planning a second one. As a result of their study on love, many members were taking steps toward becoming more loving in their families, with their fellow members, with visitors, to new church members, as well as others they had identified in their "love connections." Already reports were coming back of exciting benefits.

"Chuck, I've got to talk to you." Chuck's reminiscing was interrupted by his neighbor. Ken was dressed in a *white shirt and tie. "And, you've got to promise you'll keep this to yourself," he continued. "Don't even tell Diane."*

Chuck put down his hoe. "Ken, I won't tell a soul."

"I haven't even told Chris what I'm going to tell you.

And that's not like me, Chuck," Ken's voice cracked slightly. "I always tell her everything."

"What's wrong?" Chuck gestured for Ken to sit down.

"Chuck, you know I've been feeling kind of tired lately?"

"And you were going to see a doctor about it, right?"

Ken nodded. "And I did."

"And what did the doctor say?"

"Well, he really didn't tell me anything," answered Ken. "Instead he sent me to the University Medical Center for a complete check-up."

"And you went?"

Again Ken nodded.

"And . . . " Chuck began to realize there was something wrong, " . . . they found something you can't tell Chris?"

"Yeah, they did," said Ken, now on the verge of tears.

Chuck put his arm on his friend's shoulder.

"If the doctors are right," said Ken, having difficulty getting the words out, " . . . I'm going to die, Chuck." He began to sob.

The two men sat there without speaking. Chuck's arm around Ken's shoulder. Soon tears were running down both men's cheeks.

Ken's doctor's weren't wrong. Ken had Hodgkin's Disease—a type of cancer which affects the body's immune system. He was given about six months to live.

With Ken's consent, Chuck shared the news with the members of his church, asking for their prayer and help. The response was good, and the church began to take an active role in extending God's love to Ken and Chris. For example, the doctors said there was a slight chance that radiation therapy might slow the progress of the cancer, so church members began taking turns chauffering Ken to the Medical Center for treatments. Chuck took a turn as often as he could.

On one of these trips, Ken had been silent for most of the way. As they pulled into the driveway, he turned to Chuck. "I don't know how to thank you and the people in your church for all you're doing for Chris and me . . . we're not even members."

"We're just trying to share with you some of the love we've received from our Lord," responded Chuck.

"Well, we sure appreciate it." Ken took a breath and continued. "You know, I feel like all this love gives me a pretty good idea of what your Lord is like."

Chuck turned to Ken. He paused. "Well, if you'd be interested . . . I could give you a personal introduction."

Ken looked at Chuck for a moment. "I'm interested," he said. "Very interested."

And that was the beginning of Ken's personal relationship with Jesus Christ. It was also a special moment for Chuck, because he realized once again that this was how God communicates his love. When we love other people, they experience His love through us.

*Sharing Ken's final days was a sad but rich experi-
ence for all the members of Chuck and Diane's church.
Never before had they experienced so intensely what it
meant to "love one another" in Jesus' name. As they ral-
lied around Ken and Chris, the crisis drew the entire congregation closer to each other and to their Lord.*

*Diane spent much of her time giving what support
she could to Ken's wife, Chris. Although she hadn't yet
made a Christian commitment, Chris was deeply moved
by the love being shown to Ken and to her.*

*For a time Ken's physical condition seemed to get
better, and everyone hoped and prayed that God would
spare him. However, the doctors called it a remission,
and said it was only temporary. But temporary or not,
Ken made the most of it. He looked at each day as a special opportunity and savored every moment.*

*Since the cancer diagnosis, short walks had become
a frequent ritual for Ken and Chuck. "You know," Ken
said one day as they were walking, "I've learned so
much in the last couple months. I've learned that every
day is special. Whether it's sunshine or rain, it doesn't
really matter. I enjoy them all."*

*The men stopped. The hill they had walked up over-
looked their community. They looked silently at the
view for a moment.*

*Ken continued, "I've learned to appreciate so many
things that I used to take for granted, or never even
noticed before. Like people . . . I find I appreciate people
so much more. I used to be so critical. I never realized
how uniquely wonderful and special each person is."
He paused. "You know, Chuck, I just want to love as
many of them as I can . . . so that way they'll know how
much Jesus loves them."*

*Chuck's eyes became moist. He turned his head to
hide his show of emotion.*

And wherever Ken went, he did touch people's lives

with God's love. He continued doing so until his remission came to an end.

Six months after his initial cancer diagnosis, Ken became much worse. He was placed in a hospital, but didn't like it there. So, Chuck helped make arrangements for him to stay at home. Some of the nurses from the church set up a volunteer schedule to help take care of Ken and make him as comfortable as medically possible.

Chuck spent almost every evening with Ken, mostly reading passages from the Bible.

"The Lord is my shepherd, I shall not want; He makes me to lie down in green pastures; He leads me beside quiet waters; He restores my soul. He leads me in the paths of righteousness for His name's sake."

Ken's face was drawn and tired. The cancer had taken its toll, but his eyes glistened as he savored each word that Chuck read.

"Yea, though I walk through the valley of the shadow of death, I will fear no evil; for Thou art with me."

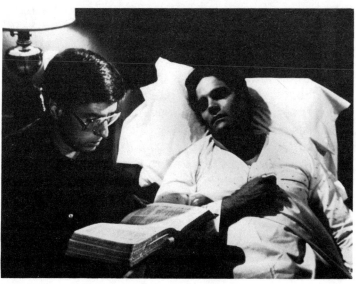

Ken slowly raised his hand and touched Chuck on the arm. "Chuck . . . He's with me." Ken's voice was barely audible. "He really is with me."

Chuck closed his Bible and gently took Ken's hand in his. Ken laid his head back on the pillow.

The sanctuary was crowded with people who had come to pay their respects to their friend and neighbor. It was the largest attendance at a funeral service in the history of the church . . . and for a person who was not even a member! Pastor Austin asked Chuck to come forward and say a few words.

"Ken's earthly life is over," Chuck began. "But he has had a profound effect on the lives of all of us who knew him."

Chuck unfolded a letter. "Before he died, Ken wrote this letter to our congregation. He wanted me to read it to you as part of this service."

Chuck struggled a moment with his composure, then began. "Dear Friends: I've done a lot of thinking, trying to sort out what's been happening to me. I still don't understand why I have cancer. More than once I have wanted to shake my fist at God and say, 'Why me?'

"But you know, it seems that whenever I indulged myself with self-pity, one of you arrived on the scene to remind me how much you love me . . . and how much God loves me!

"I want to thank each of you for the love and concern you have shown to Chris and to me these past months. In so many ways you have proven to me that you are God's people . . . people who care, and love."

Chuck couldn't keep a tear from welling in his eye and spilling over onto his cheek as he continued. "Your love was my first introduction to Jesus Christ. And now Chris has also invited Him into her life. Because of your love . . . our lives have been changed. I only wish I had more of a chance to share Jesus' love with others."

In the congregation, Chris turned to Diane. Tears were running down her cheek, too, as she reached over toward Diane and grasped her hand.

"I still don't understand about the cancer, but maybe I wouldn't have come to know Christ if it hadn't been this way. Your being with us made all the difference. I want you all to know that I love you very much. Thank you for everything. Your brother, Ken."

Chuck looked up from his letter, his voice broken with emotion. "So, who cares about love?" He paused before answering his own question. "I do."

"Is loving worth the risk?" Chuck folded the letter and put it in his pocket. "I think it is." He paused. "And even after the pain of losing a close friend, I'd gladly do it all over again."

Chuck returned to his seat.

Author's note: The story of Chuck and Diane Bradley, Ken Martin and his wife Chris, recounted in this book, is based on real life events which actually happened. We have shared this story with you because we think it illustrates what happens when we commit ourselves to becoming "delivery systems" for God's love to those around us who so desperately need it.

INTRODUCTION TO

Part Two

LOVE AND THE GREAT COMMISSION

On the night Jesus Christ was betrayed, he gave his disciples a new commandment: "love one another."[1] Not only would this fulfill the entire law, Jesus said, but it would become an identifiable feature of his followers. "By this shall all men know that you are my disciples, if you love one another."[2] The next afternoon Christ died on a Roman cross.

Shortly after his resurrection, Jesus gave his disciples a second over-arching command: "Go and make disciples!" In response, Jesus' followers shared their message of love with the world around them: " . . . and the church multiplied . . . "[3] By obeying the Lord's Great Commandment "to love," and his Great Commission "to make disciples," this loving, outreaching community of believers changed the world.

The first century Christians were neither "super-evangelists," nor "super-saints." They were simply ordinary people with a clear message and a clear mission.

The Great Commandment and the Great Commission were not seen as separate commands to be carried out independently. Rather, they were—and are—inseparably one; two sides of the same coin. The more one studies the New Testament, the more it becomes clear that the two commands are one: *to share God's love with others*. These commands that reflect the very essence of God's purpose and Christ's life must never be separated!

Look how the Great Commandment and the Great Commission are so inter-woven . . .

1. The Motivation—*God's Love for Us*

God's love for you and me, is the primary motivation behind obedience to the Great Commission. No other motivation is either adequate or effective. Only those who have experienced the loving, caring fullness of God's love will ever be effectively able to obey Christ's command to go and make disciples. The Church of Jesus Christ grows best when those who have experienced God's love respond by going and sharing it.

2. The Message—*God's Love for the World*

What is the message we proclaim in response to the Great Commission? It is the message of God's love. "God so loved the world that He gave His only Son, so that whoever believes in Him should not perish, but have everlasting life."[4] Love is the very heart of the Good News of God's message which Christ asks us to share with our world.

In the Great Commandment, the Lord instructed his followers to teach "whatsoever I have commanded you."[5] Christ's most constant command was to love; "this is my command: love each other."[6]

3. The Method—*Our Love to Those Around Us*

As strange as it may seem to us in the 20th century, the most rapid growth of the church occurred long before the advent of modern media. There was no television, radio, or printed page. First century evangels had just one medium for communicating God's Good News—love.

"If I were to speak with the combined eloquence of men and angels I should stir men like a fanfare of trumpets or the crashing of cymbals, but unless I had love, I should do nothing more."[7]

Others will never care how much we know . . . until they know how much we care.

LOVE AND YOUR CHURCH

The local church is the best possible environment to teach and practice love. Indeed, a case can be made that the single most important role of the local church is to help its members love.

Today there are some churches that are better able, than others, to equip their members to love. In our experience with a broad cross-section of churches spanning the entire Protestant spectrum, this is not just coincidence. There are important principles which, if understood and applied, can help love to flourish and grow in a local church. This second part of WHO CARES ABOUT LOVE? will give you, as a lay leader or pastor, important guidelines to help your congregation become a more caring fellowship, and a more loving church.

For want of love, a person was lost;
For want of a person, a family was lost;
For want of a family, a church was lost;
For want of a church, a community was lost;
For want of a community, a city was lost;
For want of a city, a state was lost;
For want of a state, a nation was lost.
For want of love . . .

Footnotes

1. John 15:12,17
2. John 13:35
3. Acts 6:7
4. John 3:16
5. Matthew 28:20
6. John 15:17
7. I Corinthians 13:1

CHAPTER EIGHT

Does Your Church Care About Love?

"Love is not one of the attributes of God,
it is the sum of them all."
J.M. Gibbon

Churches are living organisms. They are born, they grow, and they die. Churches have personalities. They experience good health and bad. And, like people, they have varying abilities to express love. Some make loving a priority in their church's "family life" and in their contacts with people outside the church. Other churches become caught up in the day-to-day activities of "church business," and completely overlook the issue of love. Yet, churches—like people—need love and need to learn to love.

As we consider a church's ability to love, it is important to understand that not all churches—or denominations—begin at the same place. Individual churches, and even entire denominations, are *not* equally loving . . .

■ SURVEY RESULTS

Based on the responses to the LCQ by church members, it is evident that some churches and denominations are more loving than others. For example, the ease or difficulty with which people can say "I love you" varies by denomination. Of the 39 different denominations responding, people in the Lutheran Church-Missouri Synod have the most difficulty in using these words. Members in the Assemblies of God, by contrast, find it easiest to say, "I love you." Hugging or touching among members in the Lutheran Church is also rated "very uncomfortable," compared to the Assemblies of God where it is rated "very comfortable."

In responding to the question, "How loving do you feel your church is to visitors?" members of Presbyterian churches rated themselves lowest; people in the Church of the Nazarene highest. When asked, "How loving do you feel your members are toward each other?" Southern Baptist churches rated highest among all denominations.

Is there a relationship between the ability of members in a certain denomination to express love, and the growth of that denomination? The Assemblies of God is among the fastest growing Protestant denominations, with approximately a 50% increase in the last ten years. Is it possible that this denomination, which rated high on the overall LCQ Survey, is more "tuned in" to the needs of our "high tech-high touch" society[1] than are other denominations? Or, perhaps the Assemblies' growth relates to a less inhibited expression of their faith, which includes touching, hugging, and saying "I love you"?

The Southern Baptist Convention is the largest Protestant denomination . . . and growing. They also rated far above average in their denominational love/care quotient. Could it be there is actually more love and caring found in these churches than in denominations which are not growing? Are Churches of the Nazarene (a growing denomination that rated above average on the LCQ Survey) more caring for visitors than Presbyterian churches (a declining denomination, whose love quotient was below average)? Are there certain denominational attitudes that unintentionally influence a church's ability to love?

There are many questions growing from the LCQ Survey which need further research, particularly by those denominations desiring to be obedient to the Great Commandment (to love), and the Great Commission (to make disciples).

Below is a ranked list of a few denominations' love quotient, as determined in the LCQ study, with a maximum score of 100.[2] It should be noted that this ranking is based only on the churches that responded to the LCQ survey, and should not be seen as a conclusive measure of the denomination's love quotient. Denominational bodies that wish to study their own love quotient in more detail should test a wide cross-section of congregations, reflecting the geographical, ethnic, and physical size differences which make up their fellowship.

LCQ

SOUTHERN BAPTIST	77
CHURCH OF GOD (CLEVELAND, TN)	76
FOURSQUARE GOSPEL	72
MISSIONARY CHURCH	72
ASSEMBLIES OF GOD	71
PRESBYTERIAN CHURCH IN AMERICA	70
CHURCH OF GOD (Anderson, IN)	70
CHURCH OF THE NAZARENE	69
EVANGELICAL FREE	68
FREE METHODIST	68
BAPTIST GENERAL CONFERENCE	66
CHRISTIAN CHURCH (CHURCH OF CHRIST)	65
AMERICAN BAPTIST	64

------------------------------------ median

UNITED PRESBYTERIAN IN USA	64
EPISCOPAL	63
CHRISTIAN CHURCH (DISCIPLES)	63
CHRISTIAN & MISSIONARY ALLIANCE	61
UNITED METHODIST	61
BRETHREN	60
MENNONITE	59
MORAVIAN	59
INDEPENDENT BAPTIST	58
REFORMED CHURCH IN AMERICA	57
CONSERVATIVE BAPTIST ASSOCIATION	56
LUTHERAN CHURCH—MISSOURI SYNOD	54
CHRISTIAN REFORMED	52

One unmistakable conclusion of the love research in the 168 individual churches is the direct relationship that exists between a loving church and a growing church. Each local church surveyed was asked to give its membership growth percentage rate during the last five years. In comparing growth rates with LCQ scores, it was found that growing churches showed a *significantly* higher love quotient than churches which had declined during the past five years—*regardless of denomination.* Churches that have *learned to love,* and to *share* that love are growing. Churches lacking in love are usually declining. Love, in Jesus' name, attracts people.

But what is a "loving church"?

■ SURVEY RESULTS

We asked those church members who participated in the LCQ Survey to finish the statement, "A loving church is . . . . " In reviewing individual responses, we found they could be broadly divided into two categories—"actions" and "attitudes." You will find fascinating insights on what the members of today's churches believe to be a loving church:

"A loving church is . . .

Actions
- Christ's love in action."
- a group of people whose friendliness extends beyond shaking hands at the door on Sunday morning."
- an extension and agent of God's eternal love."
- where God's love is experienced in a concrete way through His people."
- one that *shows love* and not just *talks* about it."
- people caring about people."
- a concerned, reaching-out people under God's leadership."

- where members grow as individual differences are accepted, and where distinctions of personal rights, possessions, thoughts, emotions, actions are submerged in commitment to each other and the Kingdom of God."
- a unified group of people, caring deeply for those around them."
- a church that lets Christ's love flow through it."
- one that knows the Lord and cares for every one of His people."
- where people laugh with others—not at others; cry with others—not because of others; forgive others—and are forgiven by others; love others—and are loved by others."
- one that shares God's love with all it comes in contact with."
- a church that seeks to meet the needs of those it touches."
- where the Gospel message is shared and lived."
- a community of believers who support and fellowship with one another beyond the formality of church structure."
- a church that cares enough to minister to 'the least of these.'"
- one that reaches across all barriers with the love of God."
- a community of Christians reaching within and outside of the church to glorify and serve God."
- unconditional in its acceptance of persons . . . and provides a place where there is opportunity for Christian service and ministry."

"A loving church is . . .

Attitudes
- made up of loving and caring people."
- defined by the quality of caring, not the age of the church."
- one that loves and can be loved back."

- a 'home' where one's fears, joys, yearnings, and aspirations can be shared without fear of condemnation and rejection."
- a place to find strength for daily battles, and a place to find supportive community for that struggle."
- a place for friends who can be trusted, depended upon, enjoyed, and who share the same goals."
- one that makes each person feel needed."
- First Christian Church. Amen! I love you."
- where imperfections are accepted . . . where people discover their greatest potential . . . where they feel loved."
- a warm, welcoming home for all who will come in."
- where people are open and honest with each other without the fear of being judged."
- a lot more fun than the other kind!"
- where all members of the body have a place, a sense of meaning and purpose."
- one that shares in your life."
- one body."
- as loving as its members are loving."
- one in which all are accepted and *welcomed*."
- a miniature reflection of God's great love."
- a catalyst to enable us to love others."
- one that meets people where they are and loves them as God loves them."

Assumptions About Love in the Church

As authors, we have made several important assumptions about love in the local church. Church leaders that are seeking to lead their congregations toward more intentional and effective loving, should decide if they agree . . .

1. Churches should make love a priority!

Nothing is more important to the purpose of a local church than to follow its Master's command to love . . . Love each other . . . Love the new member . . . Love the visitor . . . Love the unchurched person . . . Love the neighbor in need. When love is a priority, the church becomes an "open channel"—an effective "delivery system"—that God uses to love others.

2. Churches should be communities of love.

The story appeared in a Christian magazine of a recently converted young man who was reflecting on his former life-style. "You know," he said, "the only thing I still miss is the fellowship I used to have with all the guys down at the tavern. We used to sit around, laugh, and drink a pitcher of beer, tell stories and let our hair down. I can't find fellowship like that with Christians. I no longer have a place to admit my faults and talk about my struggles—where somebody won't preach at me and frown and quote me a verse."[3]

The church should be the best place to find authentic love in abundance. Admittedly, there are fraternal organizations, service clubs, even neighborhood bars which are more loving than some churches. However, a church which claims to be part of Christ's body on earth should be a community of love. Its love should be caring, demonstrable, unconditional, and available . . . to all who need it.

3. Churches become more loving when their members become more loving.

The local church, as the body of Christ, is comprised of individual members. When these members successfully reflect Christ's love, the entire church body becomes more reflective of that love. Church organisms are an accumulation of their individual members. Churches become more loving *only* as their members first become more loving.

4. Loving churches are growing churches.

The local congregation that prioritizes and models love . . . grows. When members know that the love in their church is genuine and unconditional, they want their family, friends, and neighbors to experience and share the same healing love. People come to experience love. Word spreads, and others come. Churches where real love is extended to newcomers and outsiders seldom have a problem with growth.

5. Love is the means of fulfilling the Great Commission.

This final assumption reiterates the basic and central purpose of Christ which we highlighted in the Introduction to Part Two of this book: *The overarching priorities for the church of Jesus Christ are "The Great Commandment" and "The Great Commission."* The Great Commandment is capsulized in Mark 12:30,31—"Love the Lord your God with all your heart and with all your soul and with all your mind and with all your strength. The second is this: Love your neighbor as yourself. There is no commandment greater than these."

The Great Commission is summarized in Matthew 28:19,20—"Therefore go and make disciples of all nations, baptizing them in the name of the Father and of the Son and of the Holy Spirit, and teach them to obey everything I have commanded you . . . "

Without love, the Great Commission "to make disciples" is the great omission. Unless love is shared with non-disciples, it becomes selfish, and stops being love at all. The *goal* is to make disciples. The *motivation* is love . . . the *message* is love . . . the *method* is love.

What Encourages Churches to Love?

While nearly every church member agrees that the church is called to be loving, what do they say about how to see this happen?

■ SURVEY RESULTS

The following question was asked in the LCQ Survey:

"What are the things that encourage a church to love?"
Here are typical comments:

"Praying for one another."
"Hugs."
"Warm handshakes."
"Smiles."
"People who listen."
"People who accept you."
"Saying, 'I love you'."
"Appreciation for a task well done."
"Welcoming visitors."
"Noticing absences."
"Being included in activities."
"Sharing."
"Remembering special occasions of members."
"Remembering me even when it's not a special occasion."
"Follow-up to needs of members."
"Helping with sick or injured parent."
"Providing meals during illness."
"Financial aid when necessary."
"Providing for physical needs."
"Sharing in work."
"Providing transportation."
"Helping family members who are in trouble."
"Helping with moving."
"Providing baby sitting."
"Mother's outings."
"Social functions."
"Fellowship groups for help and support."
"Wedding showers."
"Being friends after 12:00 Sunday afternoon."
"Housewarmings."
"Secret pals."
"Sharing produce from gardens."
"Taking vacations together."

"Opening homes on holidays."
"Real friendliness."
"Just being there."
"People who accept you."
"Respecting opinions."
"Admonition and correction in love."
"Making people feel important."

People know they are loved when they see it, experience it, feel it. Look at the *action-orientation* of these responses concerning how people know when they are loved! Recall our working definition of "love:" **doing something caring or helpful for another person, in Jesus' name, regardless of the cost or consequence to oneself.** What is your church doing to help its members see love, feel love, experience love?

Eight Reasons Why Love Should Be the Priority for Your Church

Churches without a clear understanding of their mission are often declining and/or dying churches. Every church should have a primary mission to which it feels called. For some churches, their purpose is ministry and service to present members. For some it is championing social justice. For others it is supporting overseas missionaries. The purpose of some churches is simply survival. For a few, it is building a reputation in their denomination or beyond. And there are others.

Here are eight reasons why we believe the first priority, and the central mission, for your church should be love; and why love provides the most solid foundation upon which all other subsequent ministries and priorities of the church can be built . . .

1. A loving church sees sinners repent, become Christians, and responsible church members.

Words such as "sinner," "repent," and "conversion" have

gone out of style in many churches. Yet, Scripture says
" . . . there is more rejoicing in heaven over one sinner who
repents than over ninety-nine righteous persons who do
not need to repent."[4] Love that results in people repenting
and coming to salvation is near to the heart of God. Jesus,
identifying the purpose of His coming, said, "The Son of
Man came to save what was lost."[5] Love is the motivation
for evangelism, disciple making. The power of love, which
results in love actions, provides freedom for witnessing,
freedom to be God's ambassadors in seeking the "lost," so
they might repent and become Christians and responsible
church members.

The Great Commandment is the strategy for fulfilling
the Great Commission!

2. A loving church authenticates its message.

Love talked about can be easily turned aside, but love
demonstrated is irresistable.[6]

Authenticating words with love-action was the model
of the early church. Pagans looked at the Christian community and were amazed . . . "See how they love one
another." Noted historian Adolf Harnack, in his extensive
and scholarly work on the mission and expansion of Christianity, makes a similar observation of the early church:
"What powers of attraction it [the early church] must have
exercised . . . It was this, and not any evangelist, which
proved to be the most effective missionary. In fact, we may
take it for granted that the mere existence and persistent
activity of the individual Christian communities did more
than anything else to bring about the extension of the
Christian faith."[7]

A few years ago, Marshall McLuhan popularized the
phrase, "the medium is the message."[8] His hypothesis,
simply stated, was that the way a message is communicated overshadows the content of the message. The
church which combines its message (God's love) with its

medium (modeling God's love) is a living example of the Christian gospel. Scripture says, "Faith without works is dead."[9] A paraphrase of that Scripture could be "Love without loving action is dead." The church that authenticates its message, by maximizing its love, challenges the agnostic . . . convinces the skeptic . . . witnesses to the world . . . that the message is true, not only because it is spoken, but because it is demonstrated.

3. A loving church contributes to the joy, health, and vitality of its individual members.

In the business world, the book *In Search of Excellence*[10] has caused a change in the way corporate executives view their tasks. The book discusses characteristics of America's best run companies. In the book, Lew Young, Editor-in-Chief of *Business Week* Magazine, makes the comment:

> "Probably the most important management fundamental that is being ignored today is staying close to the customer to satisfy his needs and anticipate his wants. In too many companies, the customer has become a bloody nuisance whose unpredictable behavior damages carefully made strategic plans, whose activities mess up computer operations, and who stubbornly insists that purchased products should work."[11]

The authors of *Excellence* found that the "excellent companies really are close to their customers. Other companies talk about it; the excellent companies do it."[12]

Is the business analogy too far removed from what members can and should expect from their church? A loving church is in much closer touch with the needs of its members (customers) than a non-loving church. Members today have a legitimate expectation that their needs be heard and, if possible, met by their church. Providing an environment where love grows and flourishes fills a basic need of its members.

4. A loving church attracts people.

In studying the American church during the last fourteen years, we have found that churches grow basically in two ways: through "proclamation" and through "attraction." Both are important . . . both are found in the New Testament . . . both can and should be practiced today.

Growth through "proclamation" occurs when a church intentionally conducts activities that reach out into its community with the Gospel, with the intent that people will respond, become practicing Christians, and affiliate with the church.

Growth through "attraction" occurs when a church exudes such warmth and contagious love that newcomers are attracted. Word spreads of this genuinely caring, loving body. Outsiders are welcomed, accepted, and loved. The church is attractive . . . and it grows.

In considering "proclamation" and "attraction" growth, two questions need to be asked: 1) "Which of these two growth processes has received predominant attention in evangelism literature and strategy?" and 2) "Which is the key to long-term church growth?" The answer to the first question is "proclamation." The answer to the second is "attraction."

Why is attraction the key to long-term church growth? Because it builds on itself. Today, as always, people want to be loved . . . need to be loved . . . and respond to love. They want their friends and relatives to share this same love experience. Like a magnet moving among metal filings, the church that loves attracts people.

There are many excellent church growth books to help churches grow through "proclamation." This book is dedicated to helping churches grow through "attraction." And the greatest attraction is a loving Christ communicated by an intentionally loving church—through the loving actions of its members.

■ SURVEY RESULTS

In our LCQ research, we asked the question, "On a scale of 1-10, how loving do you feel your church is to visitors?" The responses were categorized by churches according to their growth pattern over the last five years. The findings are remarkable . . .

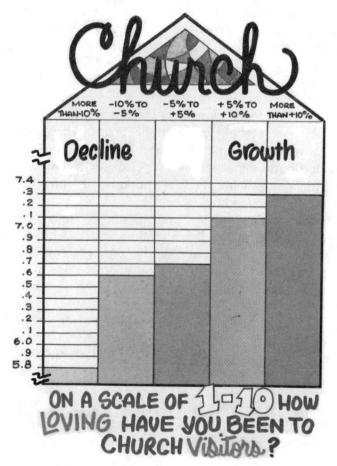

Members in declining churches rated themselves significantly lower in the love that visitors received; members in growing churches rated the love which visitors experienced as much higher. *There is a measurable difference* (as perceived by the members themselves) in the love given to outsiders from declining churches than from growing churches.

5. A loving church assimilates and holds people.

There is holding power in love. Relationships between members are closer, and more friendships are established in loving churches. A survey of over 1,600 church members asked each person how many of their closest friends attended their church and Sunday School.[13] Each person's responses were then compared to their level of church participation. A very close correlation was found between the number of best friends members identified in their church, and their own level of participation. Persons whose close friends were active in church and Sunday School also attended frequently themselves. Those with few or no close friends in their church attended less frequently, or had already dropped out.

Another study compared persons who had joined their church and were now active members, with persons who joined at the same time but had become inactive. Each group was asked to identify the number of close friends they had made in their church. Members who were active and involved listed an average of over 7 friends in their church. Those who were inactive could identify less than 2 church friends.[14]

In the church leadership newsletter, THE GROWTH REPORT, the observation is made:

"Churches concerned with reaching—and keeping—people must intentionally prioritize the development of loving, caring relationships."[15]

6. A loving church runs more smoothly.

Traveling down the road in your car at 55 miles per hour, picture what is happening inside the engine . . . cylinders are churning . . . springs are bounding . . . valves are popping . . . sparks are flying . . . wheels are turning—the car is moving. What keeps this engine working, with all the parts creating such friction and heat? It's the oil. The oil lubricates the moving parts, keeps them from over-heating and failing. Oil allows the parts to function smoothly, thus accomplishing the purpose for which the engine was made—to move the car forward.

Love causes a church to function more effectively. Love lubricates. Love reduces friction. Love increases the energy flow, thus helping to accomplish the purpose for which the church was created.

7. A loving church is obedient to God's command.

Love is not His hope or His wish. It is not an option—it is His *command*. "These things I *command*: that you love one another."[16] An obedient church loves. "By this shall all men know that you are my disciples if you love one another."[17] As the song says . . . "They will know we are Christians by our *love* . . . by our love." Obedience to this command is also evidence of being a disciple—a disciple individually, and disciples corporately.

8. A loving church is the best hope for changing our community . . . our world.

Churches, and Christians, are surrounded by injustice, oppression, and hatred caused by sin and separation from God. So were the Christians of the first century. In the midst of it, Christ demonstrated love.

As Christians work for the Kingdom of God, what is their most powerful force? LOVE! . . . love expressed individually and corporately through loving acts of a loving church. Remember . . . 'love never fails.'

The Keeper of the Springs
(A Parable)

In a world suffering from a love-famine, can the church provide a source of renewal and life?

There is an ancient story told of a small village that grew up at the base of a mountain. This village was nourished by the clear, flowing water from mountain springs that bubbled and leaped and sparkled down from the mountain to the town below. The stream twisted and turned. When rocks blocked the way, the stream found another way to bring its water to the village below. The water from these springs was their source of life.

High in the mountain lived a hermit who saw his purpose as the keeper of these mountain springs. Everyday he cleaned away debris from the springs which might pollute the water and bring harm to the people in the village below. One day the hermit became ill, and for weeks was unable to clean the springs. Little by little, debris clogged the flow . . . the water became infested . . . and its sweet taste became bitter.

In the village, children became ill, disease spread. The villagers gathered to decide what could be done. Someone remembered the old man who had kept the springs clean. A delegation was sent to find him. When they did, they nursed him back to health and the old hermit again became the "keeper of the springs" . . . and the life-giving water flowed clean and pure once more.[18]

Think of the wonderful application of this parable today. Who or what do you think is represented by . . .

- the spring? . . . Could it be Christ?
- the life-giving water? . . . Could it be LOVE?
- the keeper of the springs? . . . I believe it is the church.
- the village? . . . Those who are part of your church's life and world.

Are there ways for a church to help its members become more loving? Yes. We have suggested five important steps on the following pages. Churches that take love seriously, and want to make loving a priority, will find that these five guidelines will help them become a significantly more loving church. Each step comprises a brief chapter.

Footnotes

1. John Naisbit, *Megatrends* (New York: Warner Books, Inc., 1983), Chapter Two.
2. It is fascinating to note the relationship between a denomination's love quotient (LCQ) and its growth pattern. With only a few exceptions, denominations on the lower half of the LCQ scale are also declining in membership. Denominations with higher LCQs tend to be growing denominations.
3. Charles Swindoll, "Lessons from a Tavern" in LEADERSHIP, Vol. VI No. 1, Winter, 1985.
4. Luke 15:7
5. Matthew 18:11
6. Stanley Mooneyham in *Reader's Digest,* September, 1985, (Pleasantville, NY), p. 37.
7. Adolf Harnack, *The Mission & Expansion of Christianity* translated by James Moffatt, (New York: G.P. Putnam Sons, 1908).
8. Marshal McLuhan, *Understanding Media* (New York: New American Library, 1973).
9. James 2:17,20,26
10. Thomas J. Peters & Robert H. Waterman, *In Search of Excellence* (New York: Harper & Row Publishers, 1982).
11. Lew Young, in *In Search of Excellence* Op. Cit. p. 156.
12. Thomas J. Peters & Robert H. Waterman, Op. Cit. p. 156.
13. Warren Hartman, *Membership Trends: A Study of Growth and Decline in the United Methodist Church* (Nashville: Discipleship Resources, 1976).
14. Flavil R. Yeakley, *Why Churches Grow* (Arvada, CO: Christian Communications, 1979), p. 54.
15. The Win Arn GROWTH REPORT, published by the Institute for American Church Growth, No. 8, p. 4.
16. John 15:17
17. John 13:35
18. Another variation of this parable is told in *Mr. Jones, Meet the Master,* by Peter Marshall (Old Tappan, NJ: Revell, 1982).

Build "Love Awareness" Throughout Your Entire Congregation

"All loves should be simply stepping-stones to the love of God. So it was with me; and blessed be his name for his great goodness and mercy." Plato

A strong emphasis on love in every group and organization of your congregation is the first step toward a more loving church. Members need to be sensitized so that the love expressed through their church (and their groups) to each other, to family members, to newcomers, to the unchurched, is genuinely reflecting God's love.

The goal of loving people—"doing something caring, regardless of consequences to oneself"—must receive regular visibility and high priority in every area of the church, from the women's circle, to home Bible studies, to the choir, to Sunday School classes, to the official church board or council. Reaching out with love actions to individuals in need, should be a standing agenda item for *every* church group.

How is this "love awareness" developed?

Teach and equip. The teaching occurs in many ways . . . through sermons . . . in pastoral prayers . . . in small groups . . . during testimonials . . . in conversation . . . through the bulletin and newsletter . . . via personal letters . . . and more.

Realize that a love conscience doesn't automatically happen. In fact, the natural tendency, as churches become older, is to focus more and more on institutional needs . . . and less and less on people's needs. A love priority must be taught and re-taught, emphasized and re-emphasized until it is instilled into the very conscience of every church member.

To help church leaders build a love conscience within the congregation, we have developed a series of resources.[1] These resources, and other good study texts, can be used to provide the foundations for thinking, talking, and acting on love throughout the congregation.

Appreciate and reinforce. Pastors and church leaders can learn from the insightful psychology which the Apostle Paul used to help the early churches love more fully. His "positive reinforcement" style of encouraging, motivating, and affirming the new Christians for their growth in love must certainly have encouraged them on to greater love. Paul was aware of an important principle of behavior motivation which modern educational research has called the "self-fulfilling prophecy." According to this principle, any action is more likely to occur if others expect it to occur. Paul expected love to occur, and he said so. While people in those early churches were just as human as we, and had no doubt failed in love as often, Paul always made it a point to thank God for the progress of these new believers in the area of love:

To the church at Ephesus, Paul wrote,

"For this reason, ever since I heard about your faith in the Lord Jesus and *your love for all the saints,* I have not stopped giving thanks for you, remembering you in my prayers."[2]

"And I pray that you, *being rooted and established in love,* may have power . . . to grasp how wide and long and high and deep is the love of Christ."[3]

To the church in Thessalonica, he wrote:

"We continually remember before our God and Father your work produced by faith, *your labor prompted by love* . . . "[4]

"We ought always to thank God for you, brothers, and rightly so, because your faith is growing more and more, *and the love every one of you has for each other is increasing.*"[5]

To the churches in Galatia, he wrote,

"But the fruit of the Spirit is *love,* joy, peace, patience, kindness, goodness, faithfulness . . . "[6]

To the church in Colosse, Paul wrote,

" . . . we have heard of your faith in Christ Jesus and *of the love you have* for all the saints."[7]

Encourage love and appreciate love at every opportunity.

■ SURVEY RESULTS

Is there a difference in the love awareness in growing churches, compared to non-growing churches? Yes!

The following LCQ results identify the fascinating truth that people in growing churches experience and give love in different degrees than people in declining churches. Attitudes are different. Experiences are different. Love is different.

Responses from the 168 churches were divided into five categories according to their membership growth pattern during the previous five years:

1) churches that had declined over 10% in membership;

2) churches that had declined between 5% and 10%;

3) churches that had plateaued between 5% decline and 5% growth;

4) churches that had grown between 5% and 10%;

5) churches that had grown over 10%.

Figures, of course, do not communicate the warmth of fellowship, the caring for other people, the joy and community in the Body of Christ; but the following charts do indicate a *measurable difference* in the attitudes about love in growing and non-growing churches.

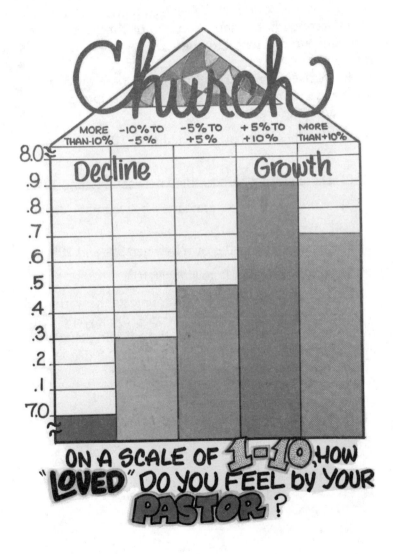

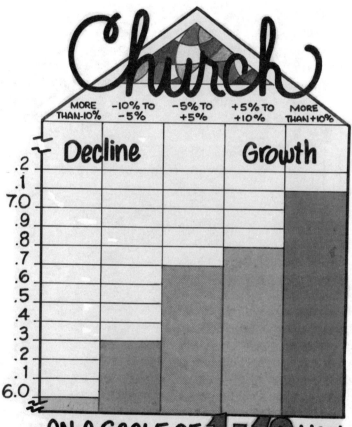

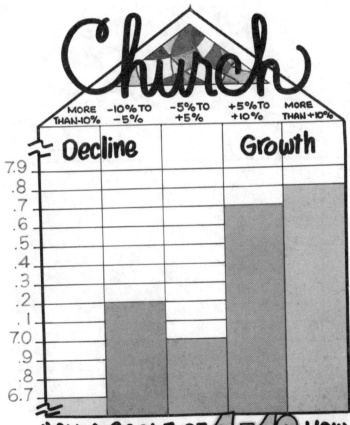

"ON A SCALE OF 1-10, HOW "LOVING" HAVE YOU BEEN TO OTHER CHURCH members?"

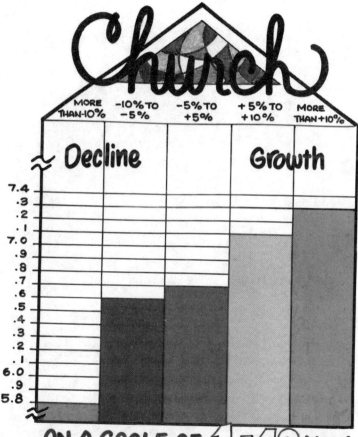

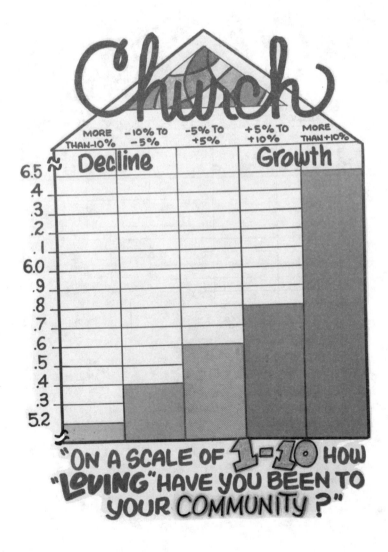

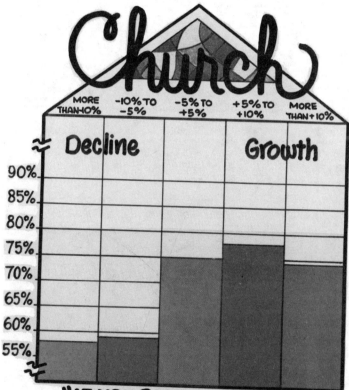

"IF YOU PARTICIPATE IN A
SUNDAY MORNING BIBLE CLASS
HOW MUCH LOVE DO YOU EXPERIENCE
FROM OTHERS IN THIS GROUP?"
(PERCENT SAY "HIGH" OR "MODERATELY HIGH")

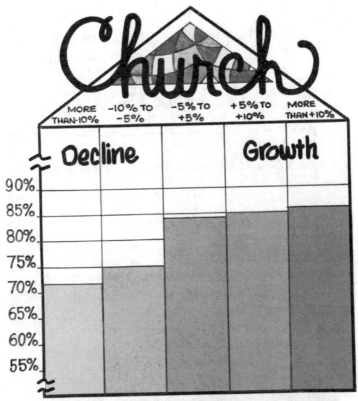

"IF YOU PARTICIPATE IN A SMALL CARING/SHARING GROUP HOW MUCH LOVE DO YOU EXPERIENCE FROM OTHERS IN THIS GROUP?"

(PERCENT SAY "HIGH" OR "MODERATELY HIGH")

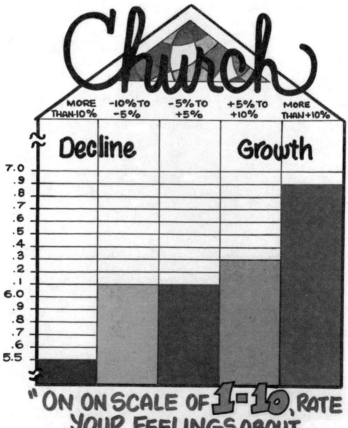

"ON ON SCALE OF 1-10, RATE YOUR FEELINGS ABOUT "HUGGING & TOUCHING" AS A WAY OF EXPRESSING LOVE."

If you were to ask your members these questions, and tabulate the results, how would your church score? Try comparing your responses to those found throughout this book, and you will learn much about the present "love awareness" in your church. Then begin planning ways to implement this first step toward a more loving church.

Footnotes

1. A free descriptive brochure is available on a 12-week study course, entitled *Growing in Love*, featuring a video tape study with Chuck Bradley, and additional leader's and student material. A catalog of other resources is also available. Write to: Church Growth, Inc., 1921 So. Myrtle Ave., Monrovia, CA 91016.
2. Ephesians 1:15-16
3. Ephesians 3:17
4. I Thessalonians 1:3
5. II Thessalonians 1:3
6. Galatians 5:22
7. Colossians 1:4

Structure Your Church to Maximize Love

"He drew a circle that shut me out; heretic, rebel, a thing to flout. But love and I had a wit to win: We drew a circle that took him in."
Edwin Markham

Does the size of a church affect its ability to provide love to its members? Yes! A fascinating observation from the LCQ study indicates there is a direct relationship between church size, and the feeling of "being loved" in that church.

■ SURVEY RESULTS

The question on the survey was: "On a scale from 1-10, how loved do you feel by your pastor? . . . by other church members?" (Note that this question correlates *size* of the church, not *growth patterns* of the church.)

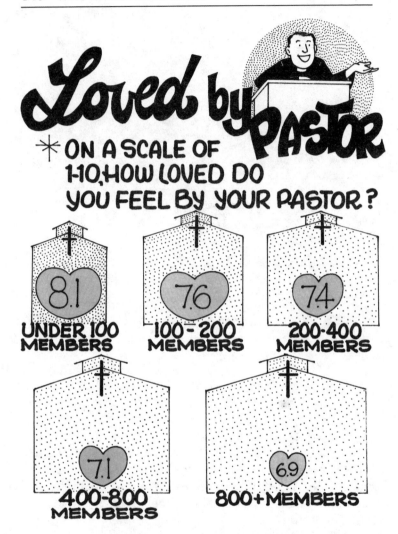

Loved by PASTOR

✳ ON A SCALE OF 1-10, HOW LOVED DO YOU FEEL BY YOUR PASTOR?

8.1 UNDER 100 MEMBERS

7.6 100-200 MEMBERS

7.4 200-400 MEMBERS

7.1 400-800 MEMBERS

6.9 800+ MEMBERS

The research clearly underscores the fact that the larger a church is, the less loved people feel by their pastor and by other members. And the conclusion is inescapable—unless appropriate steps are taken, the larger a church grows, the less love will be felt and expressed among its people. When this begins to happen,

Loved by OTHER CHURCH MEMBERS

* ON A SCALE OF 1-10, HOW LOVED DO YOU FEEL BY OTHER CHURCH MEMBERS?

7.1 UNDER 100 MEMBERS

6.8 100-200 MEMBERS

6.4 200-400 MEMBERS

6.6 400-800 MEMBERS

5.6 800+MEMBERS

the church's growth rate begins to plateau, institutionalization sets in, and stagnation and decline are not far behind. This could be one reason that churches have been shown to often have a "life cycle." As a church grows older, it tends to see a leveling off in growth, and either a long plateau or a slow decline often sets in.[1]

In separate research, another correlation has been found in churches: the larger a church grows, the higher the percentage of inactive members.[2] When we combine these two insights together, could it be that the increasing number and percentage of inactives in larger churches are those who do not feel loved by others in the congregation, or loved by the church's representative—the pastor? Indeed they are . . .

One survey of several hundred persons[3] who dropped out of United Methodist churches asked two questions: 1) "Why did you drop out?" and 2) "What would most influence your choice of a new church home?" Over 75% of the respondents said the reason they left their church was: "I did not feel anyone cared if I was there or not." In response to the second question of what would influence their choice of a new church home, more than any other reason, the drop outs said, "the friendliness of the people."

Typically, the larger a church becomes, the more structured it becomes to carry on "church business." In the process, members often come to be seen as "means" to an end, rather than "ends" in themselves. What began as a church to serve the needs of the people grows into a structure where the people are now serving the needs of the institution. This is most obvious when a larger or older church begins to decline, with symptoms of a terminal illness. Typically the concern is to "save the church," not to ask whether the church is dying because its members have stopped loving. When the church's priority moves from responding to individual needs, toward responding to institutional needs, the death of that church can be seen on the horizon.

Must the Body of Christ become increasingly loveless as it grows larger? The answer is a resounding . . . NO!

However, to overcome this natural tendency toward institutionalization, the larger church needs to be restructured. Restructured in a way that allows for and encourages the loving relationships which attracted people in the beginning.

The well-known Full Gospel Church in Korea, with a membership of over 500,000 and still growing, is effectively applying this step of "Structuring the Organization to Maximize Love." The pastor readily admits that the key to the church's growth is the large and growing network of small groups scattered throughout the city for members and non-members.[4]

"Small-church" loving relationships must be structured into the large church ministry. Any church of over 90 active members—or any church that expects to grow beyond 90 members—needs to consider restructuring for love.

What practical steps can a church take to structure, or restructure, more effectively for love?

THE SOLUTION—RATIOS

Ratios provide guidelines which can be used by congregations of any size. They provide concrete reference points to set goals, to measure present effectiveness, and to chart progress. These ratios were identified by observation and analysis of over 500 churches in the "Two-year Growth Process" available through the Institute for American Church Growth in Pasadena, CA. Computer monitoring and graphic analysis were completed every quarter on each church, and the patterns and ratios of both effective and ineffective churches were easily identified. Structuring your church on the basis of the following ratios, and reaching the goals implied within each number, will significantly enhance your relationships and encourage love.

Small Group Ratio—7:100. For every 100 members, your church should have a minimum of seven face-to-face small groups; groups where people know each other by name, know each other's family, are missed if they are absent, and identify the group as "my" group. In determining your present ratio, count your existing small groups (not including task-oriented groups, such as boards and committees, but perhaps including Sunday School classes if you believe they meet the above criteria), and then determine how many more groups should be started to reach this ratio.

New Group Ratio—1:5. Of the total number of groups in your church, one of every five should have been started within the last two years. Behind this ratio is the truth that groups close themselves off . . . they reach a "saturation point" where it is no longer possible for newcomers to find a "home" there. The history of the group is too complex, the fellowship too close, the tradition too established, the friendships too strong. New groups are the only way to accommodate new growth. New groups create new friendships . . . and new friendships become channels for new loving relationships. People (new members, older members, non-members) who are not presently active in a small church group, need a *new* group.

Pastor to People Ratio—1:150. For every 150 people in worship (thirteen years of age and above), a church should have one full-time professional program staff person. This includes professionals who are trained, gifted, and are 'pastoring' (rather than secretarial or custodial staff). If a church reaches a ratio of 1:200-1:255, growth in worship attendance will probably stop. While this 1:150 ratio may seem small, the LCQ Survey strongly documents that the larger the church, the less people feel loved by the pastor. This recommended ratio, along with others, will keep your church's "love gap" from widening. The effective and growing large church is really composed of many small churches.

Friendship Ratio—1:7. Every member should be able to

identify at least seven friends in the church. A friend is more than just an acquaintance, and goes beyond "Hello, how are you?" Friends have mutual interests and concerns, friends are in touch with each other between Sundays. This ratio is especially important for *new members within the first six months.* If new members do not establish at least seven new friends, they will often begin to drop out. Friendship becomes the channel through which love can flow. If there are strong friendships in your church, there will be strong love. The inverse is also true.

Member Contact Ratio—1:30. Each member in a church should be personally contacted at least once every thirty days—by another member—concerning personal needs or concerns where the love of Christ, expressed by God's people, can be focused. A loving church will have a strategy for both *making* the contacts, as well as *responding* to the identified needs.

Prayer Ratio—1:30. Each of your members should have the confidence that someone in the church is praying for them, specifically, at least once every thirty days. People know they are loved when their church makes a priority, month by month, to pray for their specific needs . . . problems . . . concerns . . . and thank God for their life. How might you structure for such prayer coverage? Some churches have prayer "chains;" others do so at mid-week services; still others integrate specific prayer into their small group life. There are many possibilities, but planned prayer for each member in the congregation builds mutual care and love.

Group Involvement Ratio—75:100. It is not only necessary to have *enough* groups, but also to have a large number of members participating in those groups. A goal of 75 of very 100 members involved in those groups is desirable. Participation in small group life is one of the most important steps to establishing meaningful, loving relationships in the church.

New Member/Group Involvement Ratio—9:10. The previous ratio recognizes that among your present members there are some who may not wish to become part of a group. They have been un-involved for so long that their behavior patterns are nearly unchangeable. However, this present ratio is based on the fact that new members *form* their spiritual habit patterns more easily than old members *change* their spiritual habit patterns. Every new member should be integrated into a face-to-face group within the critical first six months of their church membership.

You may find additional ratios as you prioritize love in the ministry of your church. But start with these. Do some research to first find what your present ratios are in each area. Then begin discussing how you can 1) bring your ratios up to the appropriate level, and then 2) monitor these key indicators of health, on an ongoing basis, to be certain you continue providing the structure that allows strong relationships and genuine love to flourish.

Footnotes

1. Robert Orr, in "The Win Arn GROWTH REPORT" published by The Institute for American Church Growth, Pasadena, CA, Number 7, p. 1-2.
2. Lyle Schaller in lecture at Yokefellow Institute, Richmond, In.
3. Warren Hartman, *A Study of the Church School in the United Methodist Church* (Nashville: Discipleship Resources, 1972).
4. Paul Yonggi Cho, *Successful Home Cell Groups* (Plainfield, NJ: Logos International Press, 1981), p. v-vii.

Provide Opportunities to Love Through the Church

"We are shaped and fashioned by what we love." Goethe

Love, expressed in the local church, should be focused in two areas: love *to* the body (to those who are part of the present congregation), and love *through* the body (to those who are outside of Christ and/or the church).

Expressing love *to the body* encompasses much of what churches already intentionally try to do through worship, nurture, support, fellowship, study—those activities intended to help members mature, grow in Christ, and become disciples. Such activities are relatively easy for church leaders to identify and focus on, since they are concerned with people they know well . . . their own members.

Expressing love *through the body* includes such areas as missions, evangelism, ministry to the needy, etc. In our experience as church growth consultants, we find that most churches sense an obligation to express love through the body, but do not always know how to go about it. What often happens, therefore, is that love expressed **through** the body is not a major priority if measured by the time, energy, and people who participate.

When most of the love in a church is directed *to* the body, a very dangerous thing begins to happen. "Spiritual blinders," similar to those used on racing horses to keep their eyes focused in only one direction, begin to form around the eyes of members and church organizations. Soon the majority of love and caring becomes focused inwardly on existing members. Eventually it becomes self-serving. And the result is a church that closes itself off to the rest of the world.

When a church comes to love only itself, it has moved far away from the mission of Christ and the love he carried to earth from His Father. Scripture bears clear testimony: God's unswerving purpose is that lost mankind be redeemed and brought into His Church. Christ's birth, crucifixion, and resurrection were for the purpose that the lost might be saved.

Christ opened a way of salvation so that all people, everywhere, might find his love and forgiveness of sin, be reconciled to God, find new life in Christ, and become members of His Body—the Church. This primary purpose of God, proclaimed by Christ's disciples, is the motivation and power behind loving churches.

That Christ desires the redemption of lost mankind is the testimony of Scripture in its entirety. One can hardly open the New Testament without encountering this truth. Passage after passage clearly underscores God's will that all come to a knowledge of the truth. The book of Acts is the record of how those in the early church, in obedience to God's will, aligned themselves with this unswerving purpose; and the Church grew.

In the book *Growth: A New Vision for the Sunday School*[1], the distinction is made between "inward-focused" and "outward-focused" churches. In this discussion, a well-known Christian educator is quoted, illustrating an "inward-focused" attitude.

> "As the first concern of the church we must retain the nurture of the Body. For this is God's strategy . . . as we grow into His likeness, His love will motivate us, His concern energize us, and the evidence of His presence enable us to witness in power."[2]

In response to this comment, the authors said:

> "Would that this were true! Unfortunately, the belief that church growth will naturally result from personal growth and spiritual development of existing members is one of the primary reasons many churches today are declining. Such self-entered focus **does not** motivate people toward involvement in the church's mission of growth and outreach."[3]

A church should provide opportunities for expressing love—*to* the body and *through* the body—in the same proportion it believes reflects Christ's priorities. A helpful measure of how and where a church focuses its love is found in the concept of "Classes of Leaders."[4]

"Class I" leaders are the people in a church whose major efforts turn inward toward the maintenance of the existing organization. They are good people, God's people, and the church would be poor without them. They sing in the choir, teach in the Sunday School, usher at services, serve on boards, etc.

"Class II" leaders are the people in a church whose

major efforts turn outward toward unchurched persons, endeavoring to reach them for Christ and the church. Such people might serve on a community mail committee, visitation team, they might be involved in telephoning newcomers in the community, calling on people in need, etc.

A church can quickly determine its present priorities for focusing love by counting the number of people involved in Class I positions, and then counting those in Class II positions. Most churches, in so doing, discover that 95% - 98% of their energies and efforts turn inward toward themselves and their own people.

The challenge: How can we identify the people outside the church that should be the focus of our love through the body? Who are they?

Focusing Love Through the Body

In Chapter Four we identified five groups of persons on whom (as individuals) we focus our love. Now, as a corporate body, there are three specific groups of people on whom we focus our love through the church: our "potential congregation," our "neighbors," and the "unchurched nomads."

Potential Congregation

What is a "potential congregation"? A potential congregation is defined as "the cumulative group of your members' unchurched friends, relatives, and/or associates . . . those who are not presently in Christ and/or the church."[5]

In the book *The Master's Plan for Making Disciples,* we call a member's unchurched friends and relatives their "extended family."[6] The total of *all* your members' extended families makes up your church's "potential congregation."

When your church identifies its potential congregation, you will find the size of this group to be six to eight times that of your present worshiping congregation. This is because the average church member has between 6-8 people in his/her extended family.[7] Within that network of unchurched people is a great opportunity for love in Jesus' name.

The result of focusing your church's intentional love on this specific group of unchurched friends and relatives is that many of them will respond to that love, and be attracted to Christ and your church. Identifying the people in your church's potential congregation allows for specific needs to be identified, prayers offered, programs developed, and love focused from the body in a rewarding new way.

Here are a few of the benefits your church will receive in identifying its potential congregation . . .

• You provide a *clear focus* for a loving, caring ministry *through* the church. When you focus caring and love on members of your potential congregation you will see them respond and become members of your worshipping congregation, and become new disciples. These people are prime recipients, for whom your church should model God's love.

• You focus intentional love on people who are most *receptive.* These individuals have friends and relatives who are already in the church, creating a natural bridge. Our research indicates that 75%-90% of the people now active in church today came as the result of a friend or relative already in the church.[8]

• You effectively *invest your church's resources.* Good stewardship invests the church's time, money, and people in areas that bring a productive return. Good stewardship invests resources, as the parable of the talents[9] points out, in ways that multiply the resources which the Master has left in your church's care.

Neighbors

Christ said, "love your neighbor."[10] But, who is our neighbor?

When Jesus was asked the question, he responded by telling the story of the Good Samaritan . . . a story of a person who saw a human need and responded.

Paul, in writing to the church in Rome, suggested a similar definition:

"We who are strong ought to bear with the failings of the weak and not to please ourselves. Each of us should please his neighbor for his good, to build him up."[11]

The question a church must ask itself is, "Who are our neighbors, what are their needs, and how can we love them in Jesus' name with the resources we have?" A helpful tool has already been developed to identify human need. It comes from the medical community and is called a "Stress Scale." Perhaps you have seen it. But have you ever thought of this stress scale as a way to identify your "neighbors"—persons around your church who are in need?

There are growing numbers of churches focusing and organizing their intentional love, *through* the body, on people in the midst of life's particularly stressful experiences. People in need . . . of love. The love a church offers to these people must be unconditional—"no strings attached." Yet, in so doing, those who receive such unconditional love experience Christ's own love first-hand and often respond to His love by coming to Christ and the church.[12]

These "neighbors" of your church require love, from pre-schoolers to senior citizens. The five stress scales on the following pages, reprinted from the "GROWTH REPORT," are an excellent way for your church to identify your neighbors—people in need.[13]

Preschool Age

LIFE EVENT	RANK
1. Death of a parent	89
2. Divorce of parents	78
3. Marital separation of parents	74
4. Jail sentence of a parent for one year or more	67
5. Marriage of a parent to stepparent	62
6. Serious illness requiring hospitalization	59
7. Death of a brother or sister	59
8. Acquiring visible deformity	52
9. Serious illness requiring hospitalization of a parent	51
10. Birth of a brother or sister	50
11. Mother taking job	47
12. Increase in arguments between parents	44
13. Starting nursery school	42
14. Addition of a third adult to family (e.g., grandparent)	39
15. Brother or sister leaving home	39
16. Having visible congenital deformity	39
17. Increase in number of arguments with parents	39
18. Change in acceptance by peers	38
19. Death of a close friend	38
20. Serious illness requiring hospitalization of brother/sister	37
21. Father's increased absence from home	36
22. Jail sentence of a parent for 30 days or less	34
23. Discovery of being adopted	33
24. Change to new nursery school	33
25. Death of a grandparent	30
26. Outstanding personal achievement	23
27. Loss of job by a parent	23
28. Decrease in number of arguments with parents	22
29. Decrease in number of arguments between parents	21
30. Change in parents' financial status	21

Elementary School Age

LIFE EVENT	RANK
1. Death of a parent	91
2. Divorce of parents	84
3. Marital separation of parents	78
4. Acquiring physical deformity	69
5. Death of a brother or sister	68
6. Jail sentence of parent for one year or more	67
7. Marriage of a parent to stepparent	65
8. Serious illness requiring hospitalization	62
9. Becoming involved with drugs or alcohol	61
10. Having a visible congenital deformity	60
11. Failure of a grade in school	57
12. Serious illness requiring hospitalization of parent	55
13. Death of a close friend	53
14. Discovery of being an adopted child	52
15. Increase in number of arguments between parents	51
16. Change in child's acceptance by peers	51
17. Birth of a brother or sister	50
18. Increase in number of arguments with parents	47
19. Move to a new school district	46
20. Beginning school	46
21. Suspension from school	46
22. Father's increased absence from home	45
23. Mother beginning to work	44
24. Jail sentence of parent for 30 days or less	44
25. Serious illness requiring hospitalization of brother/sister	41
26. Addition of third adult to family (e.g., grandparents)	41
27. Outstanding personal achievement	39
28. Loss of job by parent	38
29. Death of a grandparent	36
30. Brother or sister leaving home	36
31. Pregnancy in unwed teenage sister	36
32. Change in parents' financial status	29
33. Beginning another school year	27
34. Decrease in number of arguments with parents	27
35. Decrease in number of arguments between parents	25
36. Becoming a full-fledged member of a church	25

Junior High Age

LIFE EVENT	RANK
1. Pregnancy out of wedlock	95
2. Death of a parent	94
3. Divorce of parents	84
4. Acquiring a visible deformity	83
5. Marital separation of parents	77
6. Jail sentence of parent for one year or more	76
7. Male partner in pregnancy out of wedlock	76
8. Death of a brother or sister	71
9. Having a visible congenital deformity	70
10. Discovery of being an adopted child	70
11. Becoming involved with drugs or alcohol	70
12. Change in child's acceptance with peers	68
13. Death of a close friend	65
14. Marriage of a parent to stepparent	63
15. Failure of a grade in school	62
16. Pregnancy in unwed teenage sister	60
17. Serious illness requiring hospitalization	57
18. Beginning to date	55
19. Suspension from school	54
20. Serious illness requiring hospitalization of a parent	54
21. Move to a new school district	52
22. Jail sentence of a parent for 30 days or less	50
23. Birth of a brother or sister	50
24. Not accepted in an extracurricular activity	48
25. Loss of job by a parent	48
26. Increase in number or arguments between parents	48
27. Breaking up with boyfriend or girlfriend	47
28. Increase in number of arguments with parents	46
29. Beginning junior high school	45
30. Outstanding personal achievement	45
31. Serious illness requiring hospitalization of brother/sister	44
32. Father's increased absence from home	42
33. Change in parents' financial status	40
34. Mother beginning to work	36
35. Death of a grandparent	35
36. Addition of a third adult to family (e.g., grandparent)	34
37. Brother or sister leaving home	33
38. Decrease in number of arguments between parents	29
39. Decrease in number of arguments with parents	29
40. Becoming a full-fledged member of a church	28

Senior High School Age

LIFE EVENT	RANK
1. Getting married	101
2. Unwed pregnancy	92
3. Death of a parent	87
4. Acquiring a visible deformity	81
5. Divorce of parents	77
6. Male partner in pregnancy out of wedlock	77
7. Becoming involved with drugs or alcohol	76
8. Jail sentence of a parent for one year or more	75
9. Marital separation of parents	69
10. Death of a brother of sister	68
11. Change in acceptance by peers	67
12. Pregnancy in unwed teenage sister	64
13. Discovery of being an adopted child	64
14. Marriage of a parent to stepparent	63
15. Death of a close friend	63
16. Having a visible congenital deformity	62
17. Serious illness requiring hospitalization	58
18. Failure of grade in school	56
19. Move to a new school district	56
20. Not accepted in an extracurricular activity	55
21. Serious illness requiring hospitalization of a parent	55
22. Jail sentence of a parent for 30 days or less	53
23. Breaking up with a boyfriend or girlfriend	53
24. Beginning to date	51
25. Suspension from school	50
26. Birth of a brother or sister	47
27. Increase in number of arguments with parents	46
28. Increase in number of arguments between parents	46
29. Loss of job by a parent	46
30. Outstanding personal achievement	46
31. Change in parents' financial status	45
32. Being accepted at a college of his/her choice	43
33. Beginning senior high school	42
34. Serious illness requiring hospitalization of brother / sister	41
35. Father's increased absence from home	38
36. Brother or sister leaving home	37
37. Death of a grandparent	36
38. Addition of third adult to family (e.g., grandparent)	34
39. Becoming a full-fledged member of a church	31
40. Decrease in number of arguments between parents	28
41. Decrease in number of arguments with parents	26
42. Mother beginning to work	26

Adult Age

LIFE EVENT	RANK
1. Death of spouse	100
2. Divorce	73
3. Marital separation	65
4. Jail term	63
5. Death of a close family member	63
6. Personal injury or illness	53
7. Marriage	50
8. Fired at work	47
9. Marital reconciliations	45
10. Retirement	45
11. Change in health of family member	44
12. Pregnancy	40
13. Sex difficulties	39
14. Gain a new family member	39
15. Business readjustment	39
16. Change in financial state	38
17. Death of a close friend	37
18. Change to different line of work	36
19. Change in number of arguments with spouse	35
20. Mortgage over $10,000	31
21. Foreclosure of mortgage or loan	30
22. Change in responsibilities at work	29
23. Son or daughter leaving home	29
24. Trouble with in-laws	29
25. Outstanding personal achievement	50
26. Wife begins or stops work	26
27. Begin or end school	26
28. Change in living conditions	25
29. Revision of personal habits	24
30. Trouble with boss	23
31. Change in work hours or conditions	20
32. Change in residence	20
33. Change in schools	20
34. Change in recreation	19
35. Change in church activities	19
36. Change in social activities	18
37. Mortgage or loan less than $10,000	17
38. Change in sleeping habits	16
39. Change in number of family get-togethers	15
40. Change in eating habits	15
41. Vacation	13
42. Christmas	12
43. Minor law violation	11

Unchurched Nomads

A *nomad* is, "the member of a people who have no fixed abode, but move about according to the food and water supply."[14] I define an "unchurched nomad" as the member of a people-group who cannot be reached by any existing church, but will only be reached through a new church created for that particular group of people.

Even the most "attractive" churches will not attract everyone in every "people group" of its community.

As we have seen, a loving, caring church attracts people. There is no question about it. But the people which that church attracts are usually the same "kind" of people as are already in the church.[15] A church will grow by attraction . . . until it hits a "wall." That wall is a different piece of the human mosaic in a community. It could be an ethnic wall, a linguistic wall, an economic wall, a racial wall, an educational wall . . . or any variety or combination of other "walls." Try as it may . . . be as attractive and intentionally loving as it might . . . a church will not significantly scale those "walls" in large numbers.

It is such "walls" where the creativity of love is vigorously tested.

How does a middle-income Anglo church, for example, express love to lower income Hispanics in its community? The church might try providing food or clothing to those in need. They might sponsor a Hispanic Sunday School class. The church might even consider hiring a Hispanic staff person. All of this is good. But significant infusion of Christ's love into that part of the human mosaic will *only occur when a new church is established* on the other side of that "wall." It will be a Hispanic church where the Gospel is heard in a language that is understood, where the cultural aspects are familiar, where the leadership is Hispanic, where the food is to their taste, and where the songs and worship fit their needs.

So, the acid test of a congregation's acts of love to the "unchurched nomads" in its community is whether they establish new churches (daughter churches) over their own "walls" to different kinds of people.

This test of cross-cultural love is in contrast to previous generations of American churches. Some years ago, the only actions a church could take to express love the "unchurched nomads" was to give heavily to world missions. If a church sent 50% or more of its offerings overseas, this was usually an indication of the church's genuine concern and caring for the people on the mission field who had no church.

But today the mission field has moved next door.

Over half the American population consider themselves "ethnics." There are 14,609,000 Hispanics . . . 354,000 Koreans . . . 361,500 Asian Indians . . . 774,700 Filipinos . . . 261,700 Vietnamese . . . 26,596,000 African Blacks . . . 1,420,400 American Indians . . . 701,100 Japanese . . . 806,100 Chinese . . . and on and on.

Unchurched nomads are not only defined ethnically, however. For example, the Southern Baptists in Texas now have at least one Baptist church in every significant community in the state. Do they feel they have accomplished their mission? By no means. Their goal is to plant 2,000 new churches in the next five years! But a major part of their focus will be toward the socio-economic unchurched nomads in the state . . . those persons who may be in an upper income level, where there is only a lower income Baptist church. Or a lower income target group where only a middle income church exists. These church leaders know they have not reached their community mosaic with only one church.

According to church growth expert Donald McGavran, "people like to become Christians without crossing barriers."[16] And those barriers (or walls) may be caused by any number of characteristics that make up the diversity of humanity around a local church. In the "Win Arn *EXECU-TIVE REPORT*," we note that "strong denominations of tomorrow will plant many new ethnic and cultural churches today."[17]

For a church to say 'I love you' to people who are ethnically different but live right next door, is often more difficult than to say 'I love you' to the same kind of people thousands of miles away. One reason is that most churches have never faced today's unique ethnic situation. Another reason is that responding to persons next door requires a greater personal price and a higher risk. The price is in time, effort, and commitment. Not that the overseas mission field is unimportant. It is. Not that world needs should be ignored. They shouldn't. But to love the people in our own backyard who are not likely to feel loved by any existing church, means establishing new congregations. This is the challenge of loving the "unchurched nomad." Remember, love does not force others to cross barriers to reach us.

Every community, if we look around, has unchurched nomads in growing numbers. The face of America is changing, as it has in every generation. And the opportunity is for love to respond.

Footnotes

1. Win Arn, Donald McGavran, Charles Arn, *Growth: A New Vision for the Sunday School* (Pasadena: Church Growth Press, 1980).
2. Lawrence O. Richards, *A Theology of Christian Education* (Grand Rapids, MI: Zondervan, 1975), 56.
3. Win Arn, et. al. Op cit. p. 41
4. For a more detailed discussion of the "Classes of Leaders," see *How to Grow a Church* by Donald McGavran and Win Arn (Ventura: Regal Books, 1973), p. 89ff.
5. For a more detailed discussion on the "Potential Congregation," see *The Master's Plan for Making Disciples* by Win Arn and Charles Arn (Pasadena: Church Growth Press, 1982) Chapter Six; and "The Win Arn GROWTH REPORT" Number 9, published by the Institute for American Church Growth.
6. Win Arn & Charles Arn, *The Master's Plan for Making Disciples* (Pasadena: Church Growth Press, 1982), p. 82.
7. Op Cit. p. 43.
8. Op Cit. p. 43.
9. Matthew 25:14-30
10. Luke 10:27
11. Romans 15:1-2
12. Flavil Yeakley, "Profile of a New Convert: Change in Life Situation," in *The Pastor's Church Growth Handbook Vol. II* edited by Win Arn (Pasadena: Church Growth Press, 1982), p. 31.
13. The Win Arn GROWTH REPORT, Number 10. Published by the Institute for American Church Growth, Pasadena, CA.
14. *Webster's New Collegiate Dictionary* (Springfield, MA: Merriam Company, 1981), p. 772.
15. For a more detailed discussion on "kinds of people" see *Our Kinds of People* by Peter Wagner, (Atlanta: John Knox Press, 1979).
16. Donald McGavran & Win Arn, *How to Grow a Church* (Ventura, CA: Regal Books, 1973), p. 44.
17. "The Win Arn Executive Report" Number 14, published by the Institute for American Church Growth, Pasadena, CA.

Provide a Place Where Everyone Can Be Loved

"The great happiness of life is the conviction that we are loved, loved for ourselves, or rather loved in spite of ourselves." Victor Hugo

Which kinds of groups in your church are most effective in providing love? . . . which are least effective? While there may be additional categories, in the LCQ study we identified three major kinds of church groups:

a. **Task oriented groups**—such as boards, choir, committees, etc.

b. **Sunday morning Bible classes**—including adult elective courses, Sunday/church school groups, age-graded classes, etc.

c. **Small (caring/sharing) groups**—such as home Bible studies, cell groups, growth groups, etc.

In our study, members were asked to respond only if they were involved in any of these groups, at least once a month.

■ SURVEY RESULTS

Question: "To what degree do you experience love from others in the group?"

KIND OF GROUP	VERY HIGH TO MODERATELY HIGH	LITTLE TO NONE
TASK-ORIENTED	74%	26%
SUNDAY MORNING BIBLE STUDY	74%	26%
SMALL CARING SHARING	85%	15%

One is impressed that involvement in any kind of church group seems to provide a place where the majority of participants experience love.

A second observation, however, is that in the task-oriented groups and the Sunday morning Bible classes, 26% of the participants (approximately one of every four) felt little or no love expressed from others in the group. In the groups more specifically focused toward caring/sharing, those persons sensing little or no love dropped to 15%. Caring/sharing groups seem to provide a better place for experiencing love than either a Sunday School class or a task-oriented group.

But it does not *have* to be that way. For example, the Parish Planning Committee at All Saints Episcopal Church in Pasadena used to meet monthly, attending to the business of the church. The meeting was from 7:30-9:30. Members would come, discuss business, and then leave. A few years ago, the chairperson suggested they try bringing a plate of food and coming an hour earlier. Attendance went up. Loving and caring went up. Now the Planning Committee has become a place of love, as well as a place of business.

The Lake Avenue Congregational Church understands the important role their Sunday School classes must play in providing love for members. It is reflected in the Christian Education purpose statement of the church: "They are to function relationally, as congregations, providing the necessary feeling of belonging and togetherness, providing social functions appropriate for each age level, providing social concern, and practical care for the members."[1]

In considering this third step of providing a place where everyone in the church can be loved, is there a relationship between the age of the member and the degree of love the person finds in smaller church groups? There seems to be.

A comparison was made, by age, of 1) those who attend Sunday morning Bible study, and 2) those who participate in a small caring/sharing group.

■ SURVEY RESULTS

Question: "To what degree do you experience love from others in your group?"

GROUPS & Love

"TO WHAT DEGREE DO YOU EXPERIENCE LOVE FROM OTHERS IN YOUR GROUP?"

	SUNDAY MORNING BIBLE STUDY	SMALL GROUPS
13-20 YRS.	59%	69%
21-35 YRS.	79%	87%
36-50 YRS.	79%	91%
51-65 YRS.	77%	97%
66+ YRS.	92%	93%

(PERCENT SAYING "HIGH" OR "MODERATELY HIGH")

People in all age groups tend to feel more loved in the small caring/sharing group than in the Sunday morning Bible study (except for 66 + years, where it is quite high in both). Note that those over 66 years of age feel significantly more loved and cared for than the teenagers surveyed, regardless of the kind of group. Could this be one reason many churches tend to have a higher percentage of older adults who are active . . . and have difficulty attracting and/or keeping young people?

Note that although either a small group or a Sunday School class appears to meet significant relational needs for persons over 66 years of age, this is not the case for persons in lower age brackets, particularly in the youngest group. Persons who are not yet retired tend to have more diverse interests and needs, and thus it is often more difficult to provide need-meeting love with only one kind of group.

Yet, a common characteristic of growing churches today is that they do, in fact, attract a large percentage of young people.[2] Through whatever means, these churches have found a way to provide the love that younger people are seeking, but seldom find. Youth can be attracted . . . they are attracted by love.

Let's examine the issue of "experiencing love" in the church from several other perspectives . . .

Does the size of the surrounding community have an influence on the degree of love people experience in a smaller group?

■ SURVEY RESULTS

Question: "To what degree do you experience love from others in your group?"

| | Community Size | | | | |
	5M	5M–20M	20M–50M	50M–100M	100M+
Sunday Morning Bible Study	78%	73%	75%	73%	76%
Small Group	81%	90%	81%	82%	88%

(Percent who responded "quite high" or "moderately high.")

The data seems to indicate that the size of a community whether a small rural community or a large metropolitan city, does not significantly affect the degree of love members experience in their group. But, again, regardless of the community size, people felt more loved in small groups than in their Sunday morning Bible study classes.

Do men or women experience more love in their smaller church groups?

■ SURVEY RESULTS

Question: "To what degree do you experience love from others in your group?"

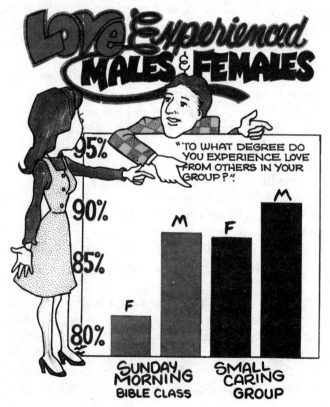

In both the Sunday Bible study and small groups, men feel more loved than women. Why? One reason may come from research, which indicates that what men expect from loving relationships is often less than what women expect.[3] Thus, it may be that while the same amount of love is provided to both men and women, men tend to benefit from that love more so than women. If it is true that men seem to be more easily satisfied than women, what a sad fact that males in society today report that they experience significantly less love than females.[4]

What does all this information mean for your church? There are two very important conclusions: 1) Give a priority to encouraging *all* members to be part of a small group where they can experience and give love (remember the need to start new groups), and 2) give a priority to love in *all* of your church groups, particularly those where it is not a normal agenda item.

The more love people experience in a smaller church group—regardless of its formal purpose—the more each member will benefit, and the more the church will be a place to *help* members . . . rather than *use* them.

The Sunday School teacher who says, "We don't have time for coffee and fellowship, we have too much material to cover," is frustrating the most important purpose of the class. Material to be covered is important, but not as important as people. In a conflict between content and caring, caring should always win.

In a recent book relating church growth principles to the Sunday School, the authors note:

"The 'belonging factor' is of major importance to understanding the process of assimilation. Sunday School leaders and teachers often assume that the primary function of their Sunday School is to teach the Bible. They believe the Sunday School's greatest contribution to the Body is biblical literacy and application of biblical truth. While this is certainly a major contribution of the Sunday School, the primary factors which affect people's continued participation and involvement in their Sunday School are relationships with others, their sense of belonging, and social fellowship."[5]

The board or committee chairperson is on target who says, "Before we get down to business, could we take time to have each of you share the important happenings in your lives."

The choir director is on key who says, "We are going to stop now for a time of sharing and prayer for each other."

In the women's group, time is well spent when one lady says, "Did you hear about the Smith's in our church?" and the second lady responds, "Yes, and I think we can love and help them by . . . "

To give love a priority in *every* group and organization within the church—by taking time for caring, support, and friendship—should be agreed upon by every group president/chairperson as one of the most significant purposes of that group. Dismiss or re-educate the leader who says, "We don't have enough time for that. We have work to get done."

Giving love a priority will result in more loyalty to the group and the church, better inter-personal relationships between members, more frequent attendance at all church events, and lasting benefits to the greater body. God's work, in the final analysis, is people. Keep that balance and give love a priority in all groups!

Footnotes

1. "Lake Avenue Philosophy of Ministry" (Lake Avenue Congregational Church, Pasadena, CA).
2. Jack Sims, "Special Report: The Baby Boom Church" in *Church Business Report,* 1983.
3. Joel D. Block, "Girlfriends Through the Years," in *USA Today* October 15, 1985, p. 50.
4. Lillian Rubin, *Friends: The Role of Friendship in Our Lives* (New York: Harper & Row, 1985).
5. Win Arn, Donald McGavran, Charles Arn, *Growth: A New Vision for the Sunday School* (Pasadena, CA: Church Growth Press, 1980), p. 94.

Create Opportunities to Build Friendships

"I no longer call you servants, because a servant does not know his master's business. Instead, I have called you friends, for everything that I learned from my Father I have made known to you." **Jesus**

Is there one *most* important reason people remain active in their church, or drop out? Yes.

While research has identified a variety of effective strategies for caring and keeping members, the most consistently important factor to members' involvement level is "the friendship factor."[1]

The depth of friendships your members have—or don't have—with others in the church seems to be the most important ingredient in predicting whether they will become active contributing members or fall into inactivity. The more close friends a person has in the church, and the stronger those relationships are, the more likely that person is to be an active, responsible member. The fewer friendships a person has in the congregation, and/or the less meaningful those friendships are, the more likely that person is to drop out.

Below is a research comparison between 50 people who are now active members, 50 who are now inactive members, and the number of new friends in the church each could identify six months after becoming a member. The results are startling . . .

Number of New Friends in the Church	0	1	2	3	4	5	6	7	8	9+
Actives	0	0	0	1	2	2	8	13	12	12
Drop-outs	8	13	14	8	4	2	1	0	0	0

Look at the difference. In the group of fifty active members; eight persons had made six new friends; thirteen had made seven new friends; twelve had made eight new friends; and twelve had made nine or more new friends.

What a contrast to the inactive members. Eight of the fifty could identify *no* new friends made in the first six months; thirteen could list only one; fourteen made two new friends. None of the members in this group had made any more than six new friends. The result? They dropped out! [2]

Churches endeavoring to increase the "love level" in their congregations will focus on the "friendship factor" as an important part of their strategies.

What can be done to see the friendships of members grow? Here are a few ideas:

The initial six months of a new member's church life are critical. If meaningful friendships are established early in this six month period, the new member will probably establish deep roots. Encouraging relationships, particularly among newcomers, needs to be a major priority from the very outset. Many churches realize this truth and develop strategies to build friendships with people even *before* they join.

Another suggestion is to provide a variety of activities to encourage friendships among members. Organize "fun" activities, such as going to a ball game, a progressive dinner, a weekend mountain retreat. There are many creative ways to encourage and build relationships. It's important that both old and new members, and even potential new members, are in attendance.

Some churches are using "Sponsor programs" successfully, which match a new member with an established member who both have common interests. Such a "match" may become the basis for a genuine and lasting friendship. In sponsor programs that are effective, the established member is expected to make at least weekly contact with the newcomer and to plan regular social outings together with other members and friends. When church activities are on the calendar, the sponsor sees that the newcomer is specifically invited, and intentionally involved. A monthly follow-up contact with each sponsor is necessary to evaluate the progress of the new member's involvement.

In building relationships, it is particularly valuable for members to spend time together in activities not sponsored by the church. Getting together just because they enjoy being together shows this friendship and love goes beyond "church duty." If members see each other only at church functions, it creates a mental mind-set that says, "these are only church friends, not everyday friends."

One of the best ways to build a friendship is over a meal. Encourage your members to have lunch together during the week. Dinners at home are an excellent way to strengthen friendships. In his book *THE FRIENDSHIP FACTOR*, McGinnis says, "It is no accident that so many important encounters occurred between Jesus and His friends when they were at the table. There is something almost sacramental about breaking bread with one another."[3]

Scripture speaks often about the importance of friendships. In the Gospels, Jesus spoke of the important love
between friends when he said, "Greater love has no man
than he lay down his life for his friends."[4] Later, he calls us
his friends when he says, "You are my friends if you obey
my commandment . . . this is my command, that you love
one another."[5] In First John we read, "If we are living in the
light of God's presence, just as Christ does, then we have
wonderful fellowship and joy with each other."[6]

A helpful resource for churches has been developed by
Church Growth in Pasadena, CA, called "A Celebration of
Friendship."[7] It focuses on a special Sunday when a church
plans and conducts a celebration, to which members are
encouraged to invite and bring an unchurched friend. The
church gives visitors an attractive booklet entitled,
"Friendship—A Gift of Love." This booklet presents a
heart-warming message from one friend to another. With
the publisher's permission, we have reprinted a portion of
this booklet for you below.

> "I'm not sure if I've ever told you, but our friend-
> ship is very important to me. Through our friendship,
> you have invited me to be a special part of your life.
> That makes me feel special. And because I respect
> you so much, being part of your life is a very special
> honor.
>
> "I, too, have invited you into my life . . . to know
> the real me. A lot of people see only one side of me.
> That's the side they see at work. The side that comes
> to Sunday church services. And the side that gives
> people the impression that I 'have it all together.' But
> you see the other side. You see the inside. The place
> where the child in me lives. The place where I hurt.
> And the place where I celebrate. I feel good about our
> friendship, because you help the soul living inside
> there mature into what God wants His child to be.

"I'm glad we can share our sadness with each other. But we also share our joy. I think laughter and happiness are the nourishment of friendship. And thankfully ours is very healthy! I love our relaxed, whimsical, almost childlike times when we celebrate friendship by sharing our joy.

"Another reason your friendship is important to me is that you make me feel 'real.' Some people think my thoughts, my fears, my perceptions are silly or insignificant. But I remember when you said to me, 'If you feel that way, it's real to you.' Your acknowledgment gives me the freedom to talk about my feelings, to deal with my fears, and to search for truth.

"You make me feel real when you listen to me. In fact, you do much more than listen. You hear. You don't judge my feelings. You don't preconceive my thoughts. You seem to listen with your heart, and try to hear the message on my heart. Those are the times when we can talk and learn and help one another grow. I remember the words of our pastor, 'A friend is someone who believes in us . . . so we can believe in ourselves.' Thank you for being my friend. Thank you for giving so much of yourself to me, for being a part of my life, and letting me be a part of yours. It's a blessing to sign this letter as . . .

Your Friend."

Genuine and lasting friendships . . . are they growing among your members? How many "real friends" in the church could be identified by each of your members? Try asking them in the coming month. The answers will give you an immediate clue as to those persons who are well integrated into the church's family life, and those who are still on the fringes. The love your members enjoy in their church tomorrow depends on the friendships they make today.

In this and the previous four chapters, we have focused on practical steps for maximizing your church's love potential. The steps are not "ivory tower" theory. They are practical steps that many churches are already successfully implementing. They are guidelines which can be integrated into any congregation that wants to increase its love effectiveness and help its members find the joy of life that only love can bring.

The next step is up to you! We urge you to begin.

Footnotes

1. The Win Arn GROWTH REPORT, "Relationships: The Glue That Holds a Church Together," Number 8, p. 4, published by the Institute for American Church Growth, Pasadena, CA.
2. Charles Arn, "The Friendship Factor," in Church Growth: America, May/June, 1981, p. 13.
3. Alan Loy McGinnis, *The Friendship Factor* (Minneapolis: Augsburg Publishing House, 1979), p. 54.
4. John 15:13
5. John 15:15-17
6. I John 1:7
7. The entire "Celebration of Friendship" kit is available from Church Growth, 1921 So. Myrtle Ave., Monrovia, CA 91016.

CHAPTER FOURTEEN

Learning to Love Again

"Faith, like light should always be simple and unbending; while love, like warmth, should beam forth on every side and bend to every necessity of our brethren." Martin Luther

In the New Testament is a rather sad story about a church and people . . . that stopped loving. Apparently it didn't happen intentionally. Perhaps few of them were even aware that their love was fading. The church continued to diligently uphold the doctrines of the faith, as it overcame difficulty and persecution in a city that was a loading port for Christian prisoners bound for the Coliseum in Rome. This church was one of the first established in Asia Minor. It had become a respected and influential church in its day, and had helped establish a number of other churches in nearby cities. It was the New Testament equivalent of the prestigious "First Church" of today.

Do you know which church it was?

At one time this church had a reputation for its outstanding love. The Apostle Paul had once commended this congregation by saying, " . . . ever since I heard about your faith in the Lord Jesus and your love for all the saints, I have not stopped giving thanks for you . . . "[1] But while it had continued in its faith, purity, and doctrine, somehow and somewhere this church had lost its most vital quality—love. The Apostle John who, in his final years of life, considered this his home church, must have been especially grieved as he communicated God's message to this church:

> "I know how hard you have worked and what you have endured. I know that you will not tolerate wicked men. I know your powers of endurance . . . how you have suffered . . . and have not grown weary. But . . . you do not love as you did at first. Think, from what a height you have fallen. Repent and live as you did at first."[2]

It happens gradually and, for the most part, unintentionally. It can happen to churches, to families, to individuals. The warmth and the intensity of our love can flicker and grow dim. As the Apostle John says, we do not love as we did at first.

What about you, and the members in your church? Are you like the Ephesian church in its glorious years of living and loving? Are people being contagiously attracted to Christ through your love? Would God's words to you be those which Paul wrote to this early church: " . . . I have heard about your love, and I rejoice"?

Or is the love in your church flickering . . . growing dim? Are you like the Ephesian church in its later years of love lost? Would God's words to you be similar to this church when its heart had hardened: " . . . you do not love as you did at first"?

But, should we even be concerned? Is not the fading of love inevitable and even normal in a church, or in individuals? Is faded love really anything more than proof that "the honeymoon is over?"

John's letter, in the book of Revelation to the church at

Ephesus, seems to suggest that we should be very concerned.

Many of us have experienced first hand those church fellowships where love was so vibrant and alive that people didn't want to leave after the service. We have shared or witnessed the exhilarating love of the newly married couple. Some of us have cried tears of joy after the birth of a child. How can love of this magnitude be lost? How can it be restored?

Why Love Grows Dim . . .

The fading of love in churches, families, and individual lives, is not usually because of activities that are unwholesome or diabolical. Indeed, it is a strange paradox that what usually causes us to drift away from love are the things which are seemingly quite necessary and important in life. And, on the surface, these things seem quite unrelated to our ability or inability to love.

In the church . . . we become caught up with concern over internal matters, caring for property, finances, program planning, and conducting church activities. In the home . . . we become caught up with earning a living, going to school, feeding our families, and maintaining our house. All of these things are certainly important, worthwhile, and necessary.

However, whether in church or at home, it is easy to lose our perspective and forget what originally brought us together.

The *only* reason for maintaining a church organization and property is to better share intentional love with people. Similarly, the only real reason for maintaining and supporting a home and family is to provide an environment to love and care for each other. But when the immediate concerns of everyday life move up to a higher priority than our first love, we inadvertently become facilitators of the very "love famine" spoken of in the Introduction to this book. Those around us become emotionally and spiritually malnourished. And so do we.

Once set in motion, this "love famine" becomes a perpetual, vicious cycle: The less we love, the less those around us experience love. The less others are loved, the less they are able to return love . . . and the less we all experience love. Becoming caught in this cycle increases our frustration and diminishes our ability to love.

How does a church . . . how do individuals . . . interrupt and stop this loveless cycle? How do we regain our perspective? How do we return to living and loving as we did at first?

Three Steps for Returning to Love

The Apostle John, in writing to the church at Ephesus that had forgotten how to love, gave three simple steps: "Remember from what you have fallen, repent, and live as you did at first."[3]

1. Remember.
Recall the past with thanksgiving.

A young couple I know had decided their marriage was at an end. The relationship had lost its original vitality. Their love had cooled. Separation and divorce seemed inevitable.

A Christian marriage counselor suggested that before finalizing their breakup, the husband and wife each make a list of all the good things which their marriage had given them. Then they were to share their lists, and thank God and each other for every good thing. As the couple did so, they began to recall the loving, caring relationship they previously had together. This became the first step in rebuilding the marriage, and successfully restoring the love they once knew.

"Remember the height from which you have fallen." This, says John, is the first step towards recovering the ability to "love as you did at first." Look back on your past experiences—as a church, as a family, as an individual—of receiving and experiencing God's love. Thank Him for His blessings of the past, for His love shown in the yesterdays of your life. Then thank your church, your family, your friends for the love you have received from them.

2. Repent

In its common usage today, the word "repent" means: feeling regret for what one has done or failed to do. The original meaning of the word is: to reverse your direction and go the other way. Combining these two definitions, the word repent means "to feel sorry enough about the direction you have been going to completely reverse that direction."

Without repentance, the self-perpetuating cycle of fading love can not be broken. Repentance is an important step towards renewing our love potential.

Repentance assumes we wish to make love *the* priority in our life . . . in our church's life. Repentance assumes that we are committed to growing in love; that our church leaders are dedicated to the priority of love. Repentance assumes that we know the cost of love, and are willing to pay it.

Repentance is an essential second step on the way to loving as we once did . . . in our churches, our families, our personal lives.

3. Renew

"Live as you did at first!"

Remember how exciting it was to meet together as a new church in the grade school auditorium? Remember how it felt to begin married life in a tiny apartment furnished mostly with orange crates and ingenuity? Perhaps you began a new company years ago in an unheated garage with folding tables and portable typewriter. However humble the beginnings, most of us have warm memories of times past when life seemed to be more of a challenge and an adventure than it is now.

Today we may worship in a beautiful sanctuary. We may live in a well-furnished home. We may work in an air conditioned office. And yet, for many of us, our lives are not as rewarding. The sense of adventure is lacking. Dependency on others—which was the incubator of love—is no longer necessary. The goals are reached. The challenge is gone. Our dreams have faded.

How do we go back to live—and love—as we did at first?

It may require a very significant change. For some churches, and for some families, it may mean changing one's life-style—radically altering the way you have become accustomed to living. However, the status quo is a difficult barrier to overcome. Even if change is for the better, most people—and most churches—prefer the security of the known rather than the uncertainty and insecurity of change and the unknown. The longer we have gone without change, as a church or as individuals, the more difficult it becomes to take the step that will cause change.

Is it possible there are some things in our church that are actually keeping us from loving—things that have come to seem almost "sacred," but have actually become obstacles to love? Maybe it's the beautiful building, of which we are all justly proud. Perhaps it is the rituals of worship, that are only familiar to those of us in the church. Maybe it's the large endowment that covers the budget deficit each year, so no one need dig too deeply into their pockets. Maybe it's the "business as usual" attitude of our church, which inhibits risk, perpetuates self-sufficiency, and reduces our dependency on love.

Elaborate programs and facilities, in some churches,

have actually grown to where they inhibit love and caring. These obstacles cause an inward-focused fixation on our own priorities, and direct our attention away from the real need of people—love.

Or, what about our family possessions? Do we own them, or do they own us . . . and keep us from a dependency on each other? The more we possess (as individuals, and as churches) the more difficult it is to love.

The rich young ruler must have been seen by those around him as a model believer. He had kept all the commandments. He had led a pure and holy life . . .

"Jesus looked at him and loved him. 'One thing you lack,' he said. 'Go and sell everything you have and give it to the poor, and you will have treasure in heaven. Then come, follow me.' When he heard this he became very sad, for he was a man of great wealth."[4] Perhaps Jesus knew that this man was "possessed" by his possessions. Could this very natural tendency for us to confuse priorities also have been in Jesus' mind when He said, "If your right eye causes you to sin, gouge it out and throw it away. It is better for you to lose one part of your body than for your whole body to be thrown into hell. And if your right hand causes you to sin, cut it off and throw it away . . . "?[5]

For some of us, as individuals and as churches, our lifestyles and possessions are keeping us from love. Love is costly. It sometimes calls us to give up those things for which we have worked so long, if they are keeping us from giving love the priority Christ demands. Loving frequently means sacrifice. And, like the rich young ruler, the price for some people and some churches is too high.

"Live your lives in love," says Paul. "The same sort of love which Christ gives us and which He perfectly expressed when He gave Himself up for us in sacrifice to God."[6]

And when we again "live our lives in love," do you know what happens? The sense of excitement and adventure returns! Love begins to grow again. It's like the long dormant seed that is exposed to soil, moisture, and sunlight. As we renew our priorities, God's love starts to grow and again begins moving freely through us, and through our church, to others.

Don't forget what love is: "Doing something caring or helpful for another person, in Jesus' name, regardless of the cost or consequence to oneself."

Make the Commitment

Make a commitment to love! Make a commitment to God . . . to yourself . . . to those around you . . . to love. It will change your life. And when you do, the results will be amazing. Love-starved friends, family members, church members, visitors will experience God's love. Lives will be changed . . . including yours! You will become God's "love delivery system." And your priorities in life will never be the same!

Remember, when it's all said and done, we don't really love anyone on our own. We serve as "channels" for God's life-changing love to us . . . and through us. That's what we, as individual Christians and collectively as Christ's Church, are called to be . . . delivery systems for love.

Our lives, and our churches, can become the "love oases" which people are attracted to, and so desperately need because of the "love famine" that surrounds us.

Love . . . delivered from God through you . . . to others . . . is the answer.

Footnotes

1. Ephesians 1:15-16
2. Revelation 2:1-7 (Phillips)
3. Revelation 2:5
4. Mark 10:21-22
5. Matthew 5:29-30
6. Ephesians 5:1 (Phillips)